Recipes for Life After

Weight-Loss Surgery

Recipes for Life After

Weight-Loss Surgery

Delicious Dishes for Nourishing the New You

Margaret M. Furtado, M.S., R.D., L.D.N.

and Lynette Schultz, L.R.C.P., R.T.

FAIR WINDS
PRESS
BEVERLY, MASSACHUSETTS

Text © 2006 by Margaret M. Furtado and Lynette Schultz

First published in the USA in 2006 by
Fair Winds Press, a member of
Quayside Publishing Group
100 Cummings Center
Suite 406-L
Beverly, MA 01915-6101

14 13 12 11 10   9 10 11 12

ISBN - 13: 978-1-59233-226-7
ISBN - 10: 1-59233-226-9

Library of Congress Cataloging-in-Publication Data
Furtado, Margaret M.
  Recipes for life after weight-loss surgery : delicious dishes for nourishing the new you / Margaret M. Furtado and Lynette Schultz.
     p. cm.
  ISBN-13: 978-1-59233-226-7
  ISBN-10: 1-59233-226-9
  1. Obesity--Surgery--Popular works. 2. Reducing diets--Recipes. I. Schultz, Lynette. II. Title.
  RD540.F95 2007
  641.5'635--dc22
                                                         2006031206

Cover design by Howard Grossman
Book design by Yee Design
Photography by Steve Galvin

Printed and bound in Singapore

Contents

Foreword 6

Introduction 8

Healthy Diet Guidelines for
All Weight-Loss Surgeries 10

CHAPTER 1 16
The Early Postoperative Nutrition Guide

CHAPTER 2 44
Breakfasts and Brunches

CHAPTER 3 73
Lunches

CHAPTER 4 92
Soups

CHAPTER 5 106
Salads

CHAPTER 6 130
Appetizers and Entertaining at Home

CHAPTER 7 148
Vegetables and Side Dishes

CHAPTER 8 170
Dry Rubs for Meats and Poultry

CHAPTER 9 175
Dinners

CHAPTER 10 228
Desserts

Index 234

Acknowledgments 239

About the Authors 240

Foreword

There have been explosive increases in both the incidence of severe obesity and bariatric surgery in the last decade. (Bariatric surgical procedures have increased more than 600 percent.) These phenomena are experienced worldwide. This massive expansion in an operative procedure in such a short time period is unprecedented in the history of medicine. It is estimated that approximately 200,000 Americans (and another 200,000 adults worldwide) will undergo a bariatric operation in 2006. This dramatic increase in operative cases is in part a testament to the safety and efficacy of the currently performed surgical procedures, including the Roux-en-Y gastric bypass, laparoscopic adjustable gastric band, and the biliopancreatic diversion (with or without duodenal switch).

Although the operative procedures are relatively safe, patients must dramatically alter their eating habits to accommodate and cooperate with the surgery to achieve meaningful and sustainable weight loss. All of the current procedures profoundly change one's eating. In all cases, patients must eat smaller portion sizes, as well as more nutritious choices to overcome the potential nutritional deficiencies that could result from the nutrient restriction, malabsorption, or food preference alterations caused by surgery. While significant eating habit changes are a reality of life for the postoperative (also called postop) bariatric patient, a major goal of the surgery is to enable the morbidly obese patient to feel "more normal," not abnormal. However, dietary changes such as these can have adverse behavioral effects and enhance the perception that the obese individual is permanently a "patient."

Recipes for Life After Weight-Loss Surgery: Delicious Dishes for Nourishing the New You, written by Margaret Furtado, a dietitian with extensive experience nutritionally caring for bariatric surgical patients, is a wonderful and novel book that attempts to support the tenet that patients should feel like normal people after surgery. This book contains hundreds of recipes for delicious dishes that cover an array of tastes for all meal times. In addition, the meals are appropriate for bariatric surgery covering the nutritional requirements for these patients. Each recipe includes the required ingredients, preparation instructions, and nutritional breakdown.

While *Recipes for Life After Weight-Loss Surgery* does not address all of the postoperative problems many patients face after surgery, it does cure the concerns about the boring or "medical-like" diets that patients often find themselves following after surgery. This book should be a staple for all bariatric surgical patients.

Scott A. Shikora, M.D, F.A.C.S.
Chief, Division of Bariatric Surgery
Tufts-New England Medical Center
Boston, Massachusetts

Introduction

Congratulations! You've made a very important decision to improve your health by having weight-loss surgery. Now it's time to use good nutrition to maximize not only your weight loss, but your health, vitality, and renewed sense of well-being. I'm happy to share my extensive nutrition background and expertise in weight-loss surgery with you, and I am thrilled you've chosen *Recipes for Life After Weight-Loss Surgery* to help guide you in this exciting new period in your life! Let's get started!

The guidelines outlined in the following pages are general instructions and suggestions that I typically provide to my patients at Tufts-New England Medical Center, based upon years of experience and input from our patients. The specific nutrition recommendations—such as calories, protein, vitamins, and minerals—are based upon the most recent research studies. However, because bariatric, or weight-loss, surgery is still a fairly new field, there may be variability among medical institutions and/or bariatric surgery teams, in terms of nutritional recommendations. Please check with your hospital's staff, including your dietitian, for your particular nutritional instructions.

The information provided in this section is general, rather than the exact diet I provide to my patients, because this book is meant to focus on our healthy recipes after your weight-loss surgery. I offer just an overview of clinical nutrition guidelines, such as foods that you may want to avoid because of common intolerances and foods you may want to eat because of vitamins and minerals that may be deficient after your surgery.

Below the title of each recipe, you will find the abbreviations GBP (gastric bypass), Band (gastric banding) and BPD (biliopancreatic diversion, with and without the duodenal switch). You will also see a designated number of weeks following each surgery category. Please let this serve as a possible guideline for when you might first try each respective recipe. However, you should always keep in mind that your individual surgical center, as well as your individual tolerances, are key in terms of when you are ready to advance your diet and the foods your body can tolerate. Please listen to your body, as well as your surgical team members, and slowly add new foods as recommended, one new food at a time to better ascertain which food(s) your body is able to digest well. When it says, for example, "Weeks 4–6 Postop," I wouldn't try that recipe until at least four weeks after your surgery. Below the title of each recipe includes eating guidelines for gastric bypass surgery (GBP), gastric banding (Band), and biliopancreatic diversion (BPD). Keep in mind that these are merely suggestions and check with your center's dietitian and team for your specific diet guidelines.

Each recipe has been carefully analyzed for its nutritional content. After each recipe, you'll find the number of calories; grams of protein and carbohydrates; total fat, saturated fat, sugars, and fiber; and milligrams of cholesterol and sodium, for each serving. I obtained this nutritional information from the Nutribase 6 Clinical nutrition software program. The nutritional analysis includes all ingredients in the recipe, except ingredients that are optional or garnishes.

As you read these guidelines, and later on the recipes, please keep in mind that everyone is different and the recommendations in this book are just suggestions. You should always refer to your doctor and weight-loss surgery team for individual guidance regarding your diet, vitamins, etc. For example, your center might recommend that you puree all of your solid foods in a blender the first weeks or even a month or more after your weight-loss surgery. Many surgical centers have different philosophies regarding advancing the diet. Please follow your center's diet instructions. You might need to wait a month or two before trying some of our recipes, but you'll get there when you're ready!

As you try the recipes, listen to your body and avoid foods that seem to be ill-tolerated (such as those that cause vomiting or chest pain). On the other hand, although many of my weight-loss surgery patients don't tolerate certain foods—such as doughy breads, rolls, pasta, and rice—you may find that you have no problem with them at all. However, the guidelines are based upon a solid nutritional foundation and general feedback from my weight-loss surgery patients regarding foods they often find hard to tolerate and those that seem to cause no problems at all. The recipes in this book were chosen based upon what most of my patients said they could tolerate. For example, I didn't think many weight-loss surgery patients could tolerate muffins, and I often discourage the doughy, high-calorie variety you might find at your local coffee shop. However, after requests from some of my surgical patients and a conference with my chef friend and coauthor, Lynette, nondoughy, healthy, tasty muffin recipes were born!

Tolerance for foods and eating after weight-loss surgery varies from one person to another, regardless of which weight-loss surgery they had. Please don't feel anxious or concerned if you find you cannot tolerate foods with which most people have no problem. We are all unique, and therefore only you can decide what feels right in your body.

Healthy Diet Guidelines for All Weight-Loss Surgeries

Before I review the nutrition guidelines following surgery, it's important to discuss the components of a healthy diet, and how it relates to your diet. The word "diet" often has some negative connotations, but here it simply refers to your new healthy eating plan. As you'll see from our recipes, healthy eating can be delicious and easy!

Fluids

It may be easy to overlook, but dehydration or suboptimal fluid intake is the most frequent commonality among patients that I see after weight-loss surgery. This is not surprising since much of the population only drinks fluids when they're thirsty, which means they're already at least a little dehydrated. I often advise my weight-loss surgery patients to aim for at least 48 ounces of total fluid per day, but preferably at least 64 ounces per day. Even then, I recommend gauging urine color (if dark yellow or concentrated, you probably need to drink more fluid). Also, if you feel dizzy when you stand or sit, or you pinch the skin on your knuckle and it takes longer to "bounce back" than it usually does, you probably need more fluid.

It's very important to drink fluids, especially after weight-loss surgery, to help flush out toxins and to help your body run efficiently overall. Every time you ingest protein, your kidneys need water to flush out the toxins from the protein.

Water is the fluid I most highly recommend to patients to drink. However, I sometimes hear from patients that water tastes "heavy" or "metallic" right after weight-loss surgery. If this is the case, adding lemon, lime, or diluting your favorite calorie-free (non-carbonated) beverage with the water may help. If it doesn't, then drink unsweetened or artificially-sweetened teas or other drinks (non-carbonated).

Juice can be dehydrating, and may even cause dumping syndrome (the sweaty, shaky, awful feeling some gastric bypass surgery patients get after eating sweets after surgery) if you drink them quickly and they're more concentrated. It's best to avoid juices altogether for weight loss, as well as overall tolerance. I don't advise more than 4 ounces of any kind of juice per day (especially not grape or cranberry juice, unless they're diet juices), since juice beverages are typically high in sugar and calories.

Caffeinated drinks, like regular coffee and tea are typically discouraged, especially right after surgery, since caffeine is a diuretic and getting enough fluid in after surgery is difficult for a lot of people. Decaffeinated coffee or tea are fine, as long as you're not adding cream or sugar (skim milk or artificial sweeteners are okay).

Carbonated beverages are also generally discouraged because they tend to cause gas and bloating, which are already an issue for many people (at least for a brief period after surgery). In addition, there is a school of thought among some surgeons and other clinicians that continuous pressure from carbonated beverages could widen the connection from the new stomach pouch to the middle part of the small intestine (among gastric bypass patients), and this could lessen the feeling of fullness, which could cause weight regain, or lessen overall weight loss.

Alcohol after weight-loss surgery is generally discouraged, especially within the first six months after surgery, since it is a diuretic. Check with your doctor regarding alcohol; he or she will likely recommend that you have only a very small amount (if any).

In some of our recipes, you will find wine in the ingredient list, since it's often used for flavor. Even though the alcohol evaporates during the cooking process, substitutions for alcohol have been provided. The flavor should be just as good, and the peace of mind of not worrying about having alcohol in the house will be priceless.

Protein

Protein will always be important in your diet, both before and after your weight-loss surgery. Your surgical center will provide you with specific guidelines for protein intake, but I generally recommend a minimum of 60-70 grams of protein per day (before and after your surgery), and higher amounts if you've had BPD surgery (up to 100 grams of protein per day may be needed). As you'll see in the clinical nutrition guidelines in Chapter 1, protein is very important for proper healing after surgery, as well as for life-long health. If you're not taking in enough protein, it could, in the long run, cause serious health problems, such as edema, or fluid build-up in the bodily tissue. Other protein deficiency-related health problems include anemia, as well as hair loss (which is often linked to rapid weight loss rather than nutritional deficiencies, but could be worsened by low protein in the diet).

In the first weeks or months after surgery, your diet may be 40 to 50 percent protein due to lower food intake overall, and the inability to eat much at one time. This higher percentage of protein early on after your weight-loss surgery is recommended in order to help you meet your body's protein needs.

Foods high in protein include egg whites, meat, chicken, fish, tofu, and dairy products. As you'll read in the following chapters, meat and chicken, especially if dry or tough, may not go down well, so you will want to make sure these foods are moist and diced rather than grilled. Some people also have a problem with lactose intolerance after gastric bypass surgery, so if you experience this (gas, bloating, and diarrhea are possible signs), try substituting low-sugar soy milk or take a lactase enzyme pill with the milk products to help your body digest the milk sugar.

Carbohydrates

In this day of low-carb dieting "carbohydrates" is almost a dirty word when it comes to diets. However, it's important for weight-loss surgery patients to incorporate healthy carbohydrates into their diets, both before and after surgery. Healthy carbs include 100 percent whole wheat bread (thin slices or toast are better tolerated than thick slices), brown rice, whole wheat pasta, and fresh fruit and vegetables. However, right after your weight loss surgery, you are typically not allowed to have these foods, since they're not well tolerated right away. Be sure to stick with foods recommended by your doctor during this time.

I generally recommend that most people include at least 40 percent of carbohydrates in their total caloric intake, both prior to surgery and for a few months after surgery to provide energy. Carbohydrates are the premiere sources of energy for the brain and the body in general, so if you're not ingesting enough carbohydrates in the months after your surgery, you may very well find that your energy is lacking, to say the least.

Sugars

You'll notice in the recipes that I've included "sugars" information. Every 4 grams of "sugars" represents 1 teaspoon (or 1 packet) of sugar.

There are varying schools of thought, but dumping syndrome may increase if you're consuming foods or beverages high in simple sugars. The term "sugars" on a nutrition label refers to simple sugars. Even if you never "dump" or had the banding surgery, which does not involve dumping risk, it's still not a bad idea to watch the sugars in your diet. I've restricted the recipes to about 15 grams of sugars or less (no more than 4 teaspoons of sugar) for general health. Your surgical center may allow you more sugar than this, but I think you'll find the recipes just as delicious without the extra sugar.

Fats

In order to have a balanced, healthy diet, try to limit fats in your diet to no more than 30 percent of your total calories. Ideally, most of the fat in your diet will come from "heart-healthy" fats, such as olive, macadamia, and peanut oils. These fats will help decrease total cholesterol and low-density lipoproteins (LDLs). Heart-healthy fats may also have a role in increasing the good cholesterol, or high-density lipoproteins (HDLs). However, please keep in mind that even healthy fats are higher in calories compared to carbohydrates and proteins. In moderation, healthy fats can be part of a healthy, balanced diet, but try to keep the overall calories from fat no greater than 30 percent, even if they're healthy fats.

The least healthy fats of all are the trans fatty acids, followed by the saturated fats. Trans fats are typically found in processed foods, such as french fries, peanut butter, crackers, and margarine. Such fats are extremely unhealthy and raise levels of bad cholesterol, so try to avoid them. (Trans fats are formed by a process known as hydrogenation, which turns the fat into a solid and is used by food manufacturers to extend the shelf life of their products.) When you look at a food label's ingredients, trans fat can be spotted by the term "partially hydrogenated."

Saturated fats are hard at room temperature, and include stick butter and margarine, bacon, and fatty cuts of meat. Saturated fats are also included in the nutrition information, so please read all labels. After a while, you'll be a pro at deciphering which foods are the best health bargains, and to which ones you just want to say "no."

Fiber

If you look at a food label, you'll see that fiber is actually included under carbohydrates in the nutrition information. However, by definition, humans do not possess the enzyme necessary to use fiber for calories or energy, which explains the recent trend to exclude fiber from the carbohydrate content of foods.

There are two kinds of fiber: soluble and insoluble. They are both important in the diet but perform different functions. How can you tell which fiber is soluble or insoluble? If you peel an apple and place the peel in a glass of water and stir it around, nothing happens (it doesn't dissolve in the water). This is an example of insoluble fiber. In general, bran and the skins and peels of fruits and vegetables contain insoluble fiber, which helps with constipation since it speeds the food through your gastrointestinal tract. If you take the pulp of an apple, on the other hand, and submerge it in water, you'll find it dissolves. This is an example of soluble fiber (e.g., apple-sauce). Soluble fiber may help with lowering cholesterol in some cases (e.g., oatmeal), and may also help if you're having diarrhea, since it is a natural stool binder.

The American Cancer Society recommends that 25 to 30 grams of fiber be included in our daily diet to potentially lower the risk for colon cancer, and possibly other cancers as well. Fiber also tends to help us feel fuller because it slows down the rate of blood sugar release and stomach emptying.

If you recently had weight-loss surgery, your center may recommend that you not include fiber in your diet during the first weeks or even months after your surgery to ensure that your new stomach and connection are working properly. Even if you did not have surgery that affects absorption (e.g., gastric banding), your surgical center may ask you not to include fiber in your diet for a while, especially after an adjustment or fill, since the narrowing from your pouch to the lower part of your stomach may be much more narrow, and too much fiber too soon may cause intolerance issues. As always, please check with your surgical center for specific dietary recommendations.

Vitamin and Minerals

Many surgical centers will do blood tests prior to your weight-loss surgery to ensure that you're in the best possible health before going into the operating room. It's not uncommon for people to have some vitamin and mineral deficiencies, so don't be alarmed if your doctor tells you that these deficiencies need to be corrected preceding surgery. I have found several studies citing Vitamin D deficiency or issues with iron, anemia, or Vitamin B12 before surgery.

It's important to take the prescription your doctor gives you to be in as good nutritional shape as possible before your life-changing weight-loss surgery. After surgery, it will be imperative to take your vitamins (with minerals) and calcium with Vitamin D, as well as any other supplements or medications prescribed for you.

If you are told that you have a vitamin or mineral deficiency after your surgery (and you've been taking all the supplements your doctor has ordered), don't be too hard on yourself. Studies show that even people who follow a healthy diet and take their recommended supplements following their surgery may have some deficiencies, so it might be that you need some additional supplementation. If not corrected right away, a Vitamin B12 deficiency may cause numbness or tingling in your fingers and memory loss. If not corrected for several weeks or months, it may even cause irreparable neurological damage. So, the benefits of repairing your deficiencies are well worth it.

CHAPTER 1

The Early Postoperative Nutrition Guide

In this chapter, I'll talk about gastric bypass surgery, gastric banding surgery, and biliopancreatic diversion, with or without a duodenal switch. Each type of surgery has slightly different nutritional requirements. Let's talk about each in turn.

Gastric Bypass Surgery

CONGRATULATIONS ON YOUR GASTRIC BYPASS (GBP) SURGERY!

Gastric bypass surgery reduces the size of your stomach so that it holds about 1 ounce instead of the usual 1 quart, making it the size of your thumb instead of the size of a football. This smaller stomach is then typically reconnected to the second part of the small intestine (the jejunum). Gastric bypass surgery can help speed up your weight loss by making it harder to eat much food at one time, and it also increases satisfaction after meals, especially in the early postoperative (also called postop) period. This slower eating helps increase the feeling of fullness and satisfaction for many gastric bypass patients, although in the first few months after this surgery you may not have any appetite at all (a good thing, many of my patients find!). This may be one of the only times in your life when you have to remind yourself to eat. This may be because of the temporary decrease of hunger hormones in the stomach because of the nature of the surgery. Some people really enjoy this honeymoon period when they feel the freedom from the incessant hunger they may have felt before the GBP surgery. Others find it hard to get all the protein necessary to heal, and they may use high-protein supplements (low in sugar and fat) to help achieve proper nutrition.

If you find yourself in the honeymoon period after your gastric bypass surgery, ensure you eat a minimum of three meals per day to help you meet your body's needs. Don't worry about not feeling hungry; enjoy this honeymoon. As long as you're drinking enough fluid and eating enough protein, you should be doing fine.

Appetite

Over time, the stomach pouch outlet (the passageway or connection from the new stomach pouch to the middle part of the small intestine) will stretch until it can hold 4 to 8 ounces, or approximately ½ to 1 cup, at one sitting. This helps to get more protein in at one time, but it may also result in an increased appetite and the end of the honeymoon period. Eating slowly and taking small bites can help you to feel more satisfied and ward off hunger. In addition, getting 48 to 64 ounces of fluid in between meals really helps.

Typically, my patients report an increasing appetite within 4 to 6 months after the surgery, although I know a few who still seem to be in the honeymoon even 2 years after their surgery. Although it may seem wonderful not to have any appetite after surgery, don't skip meals or forget to eat, because this may wreak havoc on your nutritional status and your weight loss success as well. However, by meals, I'm talking about a small light yogurt or high-protein, low-sugar shake. These meals right after weight-loss surgery may seem like snacks, but most people are not able to ingest much at one time right after surgery. Please don't push yourself to eat too much in one sitting. Listen to your body.

Your New Stomach

Your new stomach, which is about the size of an egg, may take 6 to 8 weeks to heal. To facilitate the healing process, you will progress through five diet stages, which I will talk about in detail later in this chapter. Basically, you will be on a liquid diet for 2 to 3 weeks before advancing to ground (and if necessary, pureed) foods, and finally to soft, moist, whole foods. Your meal plan will be high in protein, which is very important for healing and weight loss. Your diet needs to always be low in fat and concentrated sweets.

It's important that you eat slowly. Your meals should last for 30 minutes to an hour. It is recommended that you take about 10 minutes to eat each ounce of food (for example, one egg is 1 ounce.) Eat slowly and mindfully, taking pencil-eraser-size bites of food. Chew each bite 15 times before you swallow it. Food should be at a liquid consistency in your mouth before you swallow. Mindful eating is always a priority. Don't eat in front of the television or computer, but rather at the dinner table (ideally), and focus solely on your eating. Also, it's a good idea to put your eating utensil down in between bites, if possible for 1 to 2 minutes before taking your next bite. See how your body feels after that last bite before you go for another one. It takes your brain about 20 minutes to figure out you're full, so slow eating is important to help you avoid feeling overly full or uncomfortable.

Sip liquids slowly, between meals only, so you will still have room in your stomach for meals.

If you are experiencing any cramps, gas, or diarrhea in the early stages, you might have developed a problem digesting lactose, or milk sugar, called lactose intolerance. This is fairly common after gastric bypass surgery. I see it in about 20 percent of my patients, and it may occur because the first part of the small intestine, the duodenum, which is bypassed in gastric bypass surgery, is responsible for how your body handles sugars, including milk sugar, or lactose. Changing your diet to one that is lactose-free—avoiding milk and milk products—should alleviate the problem. If you'd rather not omit these foods or beverages, you can purchase the enzyme that digests milk sugar at your local pharmacy. This enzyme is called lactase, and taken with lactose-containing foods and beverages, it should solve the problem. In addition, you may purchase foods that have already been treated with the lactase enzyme (such as low-fat cottage cheese), so you can have your cottage cheese and eat it, too!

As you advance through the diet stages, you will always be able to consume any food or beverage you were allowed in the previous stage(s). When advancing, it's important to try only one new food at a time, so that if you don't tolerate it (for example, notice it feels stuck in your chest, even when eating slowly and mindfully), you'll be able to better determine which food was the culprit. Eliminate the offending food from your diet for a few weeks and try again.

Food Diary

Keep an accurate food diary of what you eat, how quickly or slowly you ate, and also how you tolerated the foods. You may find that you might not be able to tolerate foods that were your favorites before surgery. Many people also comment that foods taste different or that their preferences have changed. Some cite issues with the taste of water. If that happens to you, try adding lemon or lime to it.

Keeping a food diary will also help you to plan your meals and keep your nutritional goals on track. It may be helpful to review your food diary with your dietitian.

Stop When You're Full

Stop eating as soon as you feel full so that you better tolerate your food and minimize risks for chest pain or discomfort. And certainly, stop eating the instant you feel chest pressure or discomfort. If necessary, put away the food you didn't finish and eat it later. However, ensure that it isn't dried out, because that may increase the chances it will not be well-tolerated. You can add low-fat salad dressing or lime juice to leftovers to re-moisten them. Also, you could keep a bowl of hot, low-fat gravy or sauce nearby to add to your meat or chicken, for example, if it starts to get cold, tough, or both. Food tastes better hot to a lot of people, too, so you might want to make a habit of doing this for the long run.

Dumping Syndrome

Gastric bypass patients may experience something called "dumping syndrome," which occurs when a sugary food, such as syrup or a cookie, is eaten. Because the duodenum, the first part of the small intestine, is bypassed in GBP surgery, and it handles sugars, water will go rushing into the small intestine to try to lessen the concentration. When this happens, a vaso-vagal response may occur, leaving the person feeling dizzy, shaky, sweaty, and overall, very lethargic. Some of my GBP patients report that after an episode of dumping, their energy is zapped and they're too tired to do anything else. It's not a good feeling, so it's best not to see whether you can tolerate chocolate and other sweets. Although I have worked with several GBP patients who stated they didn't dump at all, others avoid sweets altogether and convince themselves they'll be ill if they eat sweets. This approach may work well for you if you're a lover of sweets. Even if you don't have dumping when you eat sugary foods or beverages, it's best to avoid them anyway. They're just empty calories and may also increase the appetite by stimulating more insulin in response to the sugar intake.

Hair Loss

Another problem that is not uncommon for gastric bypass surgery patients is hair loss. Hair loss can be caused by many things, including the stress caused by rapid weight loss or by nutritional inadequacies. This is just one more reason why it's important to meet your dietary goals. Eating enough protein, taking your vitamins (zinc and iron deficiency may cause hair loss), and drinking enough fluid may help to minimize your hair loss, if it does occur. But even if you find you are losing quite a bit of hair after surgery, many of my patients find that the cycle reverses itself within 3 to 6 months.

Decrease in Weight Loss

Gastric bypass surgery patients also often experience a slowdown in weight loss. You may find that sometimes your weight loss slows down, even just a few months after your gastric bypass surgery. It may sound counterintuitive, but you want to make sure you're eating enough. Yes, you heard right! Sometimes my patients come to see me and are a little discouraged that they've stopped losing weight a few months after their surgery, despite consuming only 500 calories. I'm not saying this happens to a lot of people, but I've had patients who were afraid to eat and felt tired all the time. When I looked at their diet, I found they were only eating chicken or turkey (and nothing else, sometimes) months after surgery. Often they complained of no energy and didn't understand why they felt this way. While I think it's always a good idea to check with your doctor at the surgery center if you're not feeling great, also check in with your dietitian to ensure you're getting enough protein and the minimum amount of nutrition to have enough energy to work, exercise, and have fun.

Our bodies are magnificent in that they will do everything they can to help us not only survive, but thrive. For example, if we're eating very little for long periods of time (such as 200 to 300 calories a day for several weeks), it's possible that the body's metabolism—the way it burns calories—could slow down, sometimes a great deal, to adjust for the decrease in calories. Ensure that you're consuming an adequate amount of calories and protein to offset the plateau and get the weight loss back on track. Another possibility when you see weight loss stop for a while is that you're losing inches, which you may not see on the scale but might see in your loose clothing or belt. Check in with your dietitian or doctor regarding whether you're eating an adequate diet after your surgery. Take your food diary to the center so they can better assess your overall dietary intake for adequacy and appropriateness.

Protein Goals

Some people have a hard time meeting their protein goals. Weighing your food on a scale after it has been cooked may better guarantee that you are meeting your protein needs. If you don't have a food scale, a regular deck of playing cards or a computer mouse can serve as size guidelines for approximately 3 ounces of protein (such as chicken and fish), which is often the goal I ask my patients to attain for lunch and dinner, at least within a couple of months of their gastric bypass surgery. But remember that you should be able to get your protein without feeling chest discomfort or vomiting, which can be potentially dangerous. If getting this in solids is hard for you, you might want to use the high-protein liquid supplements from the earlier diet stage to help you meet your protein goal. If you find you have an issue with persistent chest pain and/or vomiting, please check in with your doctor right away. Persistent vomiting is not normal after this surgery.

Exercise

If cleared by your doctor or exercise physiologist, exercise may greatly help to jumpstart your metabolism and speed up weight loss. The exercise physiologist at our center is a great asset to our patients. He often suggests walking right away after weight-loss surgery and within 5 to 6 weeks adding abdominal exercises and weight-lifting. (Please consult with your doctor before engaging in exercise after your surgery.)

Your New Body

Especially in the first few months after your weight-loss surgery, you may start to feel anxious about comments and compliments about your weight loss or your new body. You may feel uncomfortable with an enhanced amount of attention or find that new issues may replace old ones in your life as a result of your weight loss. Please know that this uneasiness is common. The decision to pursue gastric bypass surgery often involves a major change in your lifestyle, which may affect all areas of your life. Remember that you are not alone in this process. It is important to involve yourself in postoperative support groups and to meet regularly with the members of your health care team, including your nutritionist, doctor, and psychologist.

Your Diet Following Gastric Bypass Surgery

Since having your gastric bypass surgery, your stomach has been altered, in both its anatomy and function. You need to make special dietary changes to ensure successful weight loss while lowering the risk of malnutrition. In this section, I describe what happens at our center, which I hope will help you understand the various stages of your diet. Once again, you may find that your center has somewhat different guidelines. The diet after gastric bypass surgery may vary quite a bit among surgical centers. These instructions are only suggestions. Please check with your center's dietitian for your personal meal plan and pre- and postoperative nutritional instructions.

STAGE 1

DIET: 1 ounce water per hour

INSTRUCTIONS: In the hospital on the day after surgery, our patients drink 1 ounce of water per hour from a 1-ounce medicine cup. They are advised to stop sipping water if they feel nauseated. They are also told that it's not unusual to experience dry mouth, and they are given swabs to moisten their mouths.

STAGE 2

DIET: 3 fluid ounces 3 times per day

INSTRUCTIONS: In the hospital on the second day after surgery, our patients are given 3 fluid ounces of diet gelatin and chicken or beef bullion 3 times per day. Between these meals, our patients are allowed to sip water or flattened diet ginger ale.

Flattened diet carbonated beverages are okay, but we discourage drinking regular, unflattened carbonated beverages because they may cause a great deal of gas to become trapped in the connection (or anastomoses) where the new stomach pouch meets the middle part of the small intestine. This gas bloat may cause a great deal of discomfort. Also, it's possible that continued increased pressure in the new connection (anastomosis) from chronic use of carbonated beverages after gastric bypass surgery could stretch this outlet and cause a decreased feeling of fullness, which could lessen weight loss and/or cause weight regain after GBP surgery. It's not proven, but why risk stretching out your new connection from your pouch?

We encourage our patients to stop sipping or eating as soon as they feel full or nauseated. They are advised to drink slowly, and not to gulp fluids.

Our patients are also encouraged to walk as much as they can, even while in the hospital. Often our patients will walk down the hospital halls with their nurse and/or a friend. This is really key to get the blood circulating and possibly decrease your risk of getting a blood clot after surgery. (This risk is not unique to weight-loss surgery. If you're not moving or walking after just about any kind of surgery, you could be at risk for a blood clot, according to many doctors with whom I've talked.) If you feel pain, weakness, or dizziness, of course you should stop, but if you feel good, walking could also help get rid of postoperative gas pain and discomfort. Sometimes I see my GBP patients walking at a pretty good clip! (Check with your doctor before starting to exercise, including walking, after your surgery.)

At the two-week postop visit, which is usually when our patients begin stage 4, they start taking a chewable multivitamin/mineral supplement. They take either 1 adult chewable vitamin or 1½ to 2 children's chewable vitamins.

Also at this time, we recommend our patients begin taking calcium supplements, 600 milligrams 2 or 3 times per day. But because our bodies can only absorb 600 milligrams of calcium at one time, you need to space your calcium tablets at least a few hours apart. Also, don't take calcium at the same time as your multivitamin because the iron in the multivitamin may decrease the absorption of the calcium. There are several types of calcium supplements, including calcium citrate and calcium carbonate. Calcium citrate is preferable to calcium carbonate because calcium carbonate requires stomach acid for your body to absorb it. Since you don't have much acid left in your pouch after GBP surgery, you may not have very good absorption of the calcium carbonate.

For the first 6 months following gastric bypass surgery, our patients are on antacid therapy. This helps prevent ulcers and other problems. I advise my patients not to take calcium carbonate at the same time as the antacid, because the antacid will decrease stomach acid, which the calcium carbonate needs to be absorbed.

Here's a sample day in the later stages of the postop gastric bypass surgery diet, 6 weeks or more after surgery:

BREAKFAST

1 whole egg, preferably using a cooking spray rather than oil, butter, or margarine to keep the fat in the diet low and help improve tolerance in the early days after your gastric bypass surgery.

LUNCH

1 to 3 ounces of fish. Fish, in general, is nice and soft and high in protein, so it's generally better-tolerated than steak or a tough, grilled piece of chicken. Seafood—such as shrimp, lobster, and scallops—may be well-tolerated if moist (add lemon and lime instead of high-calorie butter) and chewed well. Shellfish, such as clams and mussels, are a bit "slimy" going down and hard to cut into pencil-eraser-sized bites, so they may not be the best choice in the early postop period, but everyone is different. I recommend people stay away from raw fish for the first month or so after surgery, just in case it's tainted. Chopsticks are a great way to help make sure you're eating slowly and mindfully.

SNACK

Low-fat, low-sugar yogurt.

DINNER

Small to medium bowl of low-fat chili or lentil soup. It's a good source of fiber; just check with your surgery center because some centers may have you puree beans, etc., for several weeks after your surgery.

SNACK

8-ounce glass of nonfat or 1% milk or a high-protein, low-sugar, low-fat liquid shake. It's a great source of calcium as well.

A few last notes about gastric bypass surgery: Please do not ever chew gum. The possible risk of obstruction or blockage is present if you swallow it. Chewing gum tends to introduce air into your body and may cause bloating and/or gas (especially with sugar-alcohol, or sorbitol-containing gums).

Keep in mind that you have what I describe to my patients as "a baby stomach in training." That is, it's tiny in area, and you may not be able to tolerate foods that never caused you problems before, such as spicy foods and lactose-containing foods and beverages. Your tastes may be very different too, so please allow your new palate to adjust to one new food at a time.

Lastly, at stage 4, you will not eat raw fruits and vegetables or starchy foods because this stage is all about protein, ideally very moist and easily-digested protein, such as lean, ground turkey with fat-free gravy on it. However, if you're climbing the walls craving vegetables, you might try homemade winter squash or mashed potatoes made with nonfat milk and treated with the lactase enzyme if milk sugar is a problem for you.

STAGE 5: LOW-FAT, LOW-SUGAR SOLID FOODS

DIET: A healthy, balanced diet of low-fat, low-sugar solid foods

DIETARY GOALS: 64 ounces or more of fluids per day and 60 to 80 grams of protein per day

INSTRUCTIONS: About 5 to 8 weeks after surgery, you will begin stage 5. Congratulations! This is the final stage. It includes fruits, vegetables, and starches, but we urge our patients to always avoid commonly ill-tolerated foods, such as doughy breads, rolls, pasta, rice, and skins, such as potato skins, apple skins, and cucumber skins.

It's very important to continue to eat slowly and mindfully. Also continue to avoid drinking fluids with meals, as well as 30 minutes before and after meals. Please make sure you add only one new food at a time to better ensure you can tolerate it. When in doubt, try only a small amount. Continue keeping your food diaries.

At stage 5, the foods that many of my patients report as problems include red meat, doughy breads, pasta, rice, tomato sauce, dry or tough chicken or turkey, and raw fruits and vegetables (the skins in particular). Easier foods to digest and tolerate in the beginning of this stage include toast, cereal, crackers, pita bread, and well-cooked vegetables and fruits.

If you're a vegetarian, especially if you're entirely vegan, check with your dietitian to better ensure you're meeting your protein needs with your vegetable sources, such as tofu, beans, and veggie burgers. But if you have a problem with excessive gas from eating beans and lentils, you can buy pills that contain natural enzymes to help you digest beans and lentils. Also, mashing the beans well may better ensure tolerance. Some commercial bean and chili dishes (especially canned) are high in sugars. Always check labels, including those of beans, to confirm that you're not consuming more than 14 grams of sugars per serving. Other commercial bean and chili dishes are high in fat. Aim for less than 5 grams of fat per serving, because fats slow down the emptying of your stomach, which is still only the size of an egg.

Incorporating All Food Groups

Here in stage 5, your dietitian can help you incorporate all of the food groups from the food guide pyramid, although the portion sizes will be smaller. The food groups include grains and starches, fruits, vegetables, protein, and dairy. Within these groups, it is important to emphasize high-protein, low-fat, low-sugar foods in order to minimize stomach upset.

Even after advancing to stage 5, the final diet stage, my patients often find it takes a month or two (and in some cases, several months) to expand their diet repertoire to include a wide variety of foods. Over time, you'll be able to tolerate more foods as well as a larger quantity at one time, because it's common for the stomach pouch outlet (new passageway from your new stomach to the middle part of the small intestine) to expand to twice the size it was right after surgery (to the size of two eggs instead of one), even if you're eating slowly and mindfully. That should make it a little easier to get the protein and other nutrients in, including fruits and vegetables, which are often filling because of their higher fiber content. Please don't drink any fluids with meals or within the first 30 minutes or so after eating to help your new pouch hold onto food longer before it empties into the new passageway. If food travels through the new passageway too fast, it could leave you feeling hungry and dissatisfied, which you don't want, because it may cause you to overeat and regain weight. It may take work to remember these tips and remain consistent, but they can help you lose weight and keep it off. I know you can do it!

Gastric Banding Surgery

CONGRATULATIONS ON YOUR GASTRIC BANDING SURGERY!

Although the anatomy of your body wasn't changed with this surgery, the silicone band you had placed in your stomach separates your stomach into two chambers, similar to an hourglass. The very small upper chamber is connected by a narrow channel to the much larger lower chamber, which includes most of your stomach's storage capacity. Because of this, food moves through your stomach more slowly.

After your initial surgery, when the surgeon placed the band near the top of your stomach, your body will need time to heal, since it typically swells a little bit during this procedure. This may leave you with little or no appetite at first.

Feeling Hungry

However, after the swelling goes down, you may feel hungry, perhaps much hungrier than you imagined you would even 1 to 2 weeks postop. Don't worry; this is why your surgeon will schedule fills or adjustments, which typically involve injections of a small amount of saline (salt solution) into your abdomen, where your "port" is located. (Your port is the spot where your surgeon or other clinician at your center will inject the salt solution in order to tighten your band and create a more narrow passageway from the top of your stomach, above your band, to the lower larger part of your stomach, below your band. Your port is about the size of a quarter, and it is under you skin, usually in the area above your belly button and just below your rib cage, although centers vary in terms of exactly where they place the port within your abdominal cavity. This is under your skin, so no one will see your port, and many of my patients tell me they can't feel it and/or it doesn't bother them.) This should cause more of a bottleneck at the top of your stomach, which should increase your feeling of fullness. After this, the small top part of your stomach will fill up faster and the large bottom part of your stomach will empty slower.

After your surgery, your diet will go through several stages, which I'll discuss in more detail later in this chapter. In order to help your tissues heal after your gastric banding surgery, your postop diet will be high in protein, and primarily liquid. Then, after two to three weeks, you should be able to advance to pureed or ground foods. (Check with your center's doctor or nutritionist regarding whether you need pureed texture.)

Changing the Way You Eat

After having gastric banding surgery, you will need to change the way you eat. Although your stomach has not been cut into two parts, the top part of your stomach, above where the band was placed, is going to do the mechanical chewing job that your whole stomach was previously doing. Because your whole stomach is about the size of a football, but the part that's now doing the work is only the size of your thumb, you will need to chew your food much more carefully to decrease the chances that food will get stuck in the narrow hourglass part where your band is sitting. That bottleneck may be as narrow as your little finger. Take pencil-eraser-size bites of food and chew each bite 15 to 25 times, until the food is a liquid consistency.

This will help to prevent food from getting "stuck" in the upper part of your stomach, just above your silicone band. If you feel intense chest pressure, pain, or experience persistent vomiting after eating a large piece of food, call your doctor.

Avoid Drinking Fluids with Meals

After your surgery, it's important not to drink fluids with meals, as well as 30 minutes after meals. Drinking fluids during and right after a meal flushes the food through the band, or backfires, and causes regurgitation. As you graduate from liquids to ground foods to soft-solids, it is very important to limit the amount of high-calorie liquids that you drink. For example, juices and soda are discouraged. Your gastric band is designed to limit the solid foods you eat rather than liquids. That means, unfortunately, that some very weight unfriendly items—such as juice, soda, milkshakes, and even ice cream—tend to go down easily, which is not a good thing for weight loss. Specifically, try to avoid soda, even diet, because it tends to cause quite a bit of gas and bloating, and drinking it may prevent you from reaching your fluid and protein goals.

Eat Slowly

Eat very slowly. It's recommended that you allow about 5 to 10 minutes for each ounce of food that you eat. (An ounce of chicken is about one-third the size of a standard deck of playing cards or a computer mouse.) That translates into about 15 to 30 minutes for a 3-ounce portion of fish, for example. It's key that you put down your eating utensil between bites. Eating slowly and mindfully may help you to better tolerate your diet and lower the risk of food getting stuck because you didn't chew thoroughly enough. Don't force yourself to finish your food within a specific time or to ingest a particular amount of food in at one sitting. You're much better off stopping your meal as soon as you feel chest fullness or pressure than continuing to eat and vomiting.

Introducing New Foods

When advancing through the dietary stages, it is important to try only one new food at a time. This way, if you don't tolerate a particular food, you'll be able to ascertain which one didn't sit well with you. Also, I always tell my patients "when in doubt, only try a small amount." That is, if you're trying a food for the first time, go with a tiny amount, like you would give a baby just starting table foods. Also, even though your stomach wasn't cut into with the gastric band, you may find that your tastes have changed and that foods you could always tolerate before are not tolerated or liked now.

Other Important Considerations

To help your body heal, it is vital that you eat a minimum of 3 protein meals per day. You may find that your new pouch may only hold only a small amount, especially after a fill or adjustment by your surgeon. Therefore, you may prefer 4 to 6 small, high-protein meals, such as light yogurt or an 8-ounce glass of nonfat or 1% milk to help you meet your protein goal. However, I typically discourage "grazing," which involves increased snacking, such as with foods like crackers, nuts, and cookies. These foods tend to go down very well, but are not nutrient-dense, nor are they very weight-friendly.

After having banding surgery, avoid chewing gum altogether. It tends to introduce a lot of air, and it may cause gas and discomfort, especially if you select one with sugar alcohols, such as sorbitol.

As you know, the band is a tool for weight loss, but is not magic that will do the work for you. You're still responsible for making healthy food choices, but the portions will be controlled by the band. Regular visits with your doctor after your band is placed can help you to achieve the optimal level of fullness with the band and better allow you to be successful in meeting your long-term weight loss goals.

Your Diet Following Gastric Banding Surgery

In this section, I describe what happens at our center, which I hope will help you understand the various stages of your diet. Once again, you may find that your center has somewhat different guidelines. The diet after gastric banding surgery may vary quite a bit among surgical centers. These instructions are only suggestions. Please check with your center's dietitian for your personal meal plan and pre- and postoperative nutritional instructions.

Because the gastric banding surgery is less invasive and complex than the gastric bypass surgery, stages 1 and 2 are combined and introduced earlier on, rather than waiting until the day after surgery.

STAGE 1

DIET: Water

INSTRUCTIONS: This stage begins in the hospital on the day of surgery, and it lasts for one day. Our patients try to sip about 1 to 4 ounces of fluid per hour, always remembering to avoid gulping. We urge them to stop if they feel full or nauseated. (Note that some surgeons don't allow their patients to even drink until the day after surgery.)

STAGE 2

DIET: Sugar-free clear liquids

INSTRUCTIONS: This stage also begins in the hospital on the day of surgery, and it lasts for two days. Patients are given sugar-free clear liquids to drink, such as beef, chicken, or vegetable broth.

Although sugars do not cause dumping among gastric banding patients like they do for gastric bypass patients, diet beverages are recommended to keep simple calories and sugars low. Some centers give their patients gelatin at this stage, but others have their patients avoid it because of its consistency. Some surgeons report patients getting dysphagia (difficulty swallowing) or even vomiting from gelatin. Check with your surgical center regarding whether it allows gelatin at this stage.

STAGE 3

DIET: Sugar-free, low-fat full liquids

DIETARY GOALS: Drink at least 64 ounces of fluid per day and eat a minimum of 50 to 60 grams of protein per day.

INSTRUCTIONS: This stage usually begins on the third day after surgery. It lasts for 2 to 3 weeks. Note that some surgical centers have their gastric banding patients stay on liquids only for 2 weeks, but others have them stay on liquids for 4 weeks after their band is placed. Please check with your center regarding your specific dietary recommendations after your banding surgery.

This stage includes high-protein, low-sugar drinks (the low sugar is for keeping empty calories low); low-fat cottage cheese; fat-free cottage cheese; egg whites; whole eggs (if desired); sugar-free, fat-free pudding; low-fat cream soups; and low-fat, low-sugar yogurt.

The most important thing at this stage, even more than getting enough protein, is getting enough fluid into your body, because dehydration is common right after surgery. This may stem from the decreased amount of time in your day for drinking because you are discouraged from drinking with meals, or 30 minutes after meals.

Sip fluids slowly over a 45- to 60-minute period (as if you are drinking hot tea). Don't gulp them. If you're drinking your goal of 64 ounces of fluid per day but find you have a very dry mouth, your urine is dark, and/or you're feeling dizzy when you stand up, you may need to increase your fluid intake further.

In order to meet your fluid goals and also your protein goals, try to drink at least 1 high-protein drink per day. These high-protein drinks are a meal, not a snack, and they could be used up to three times a day to replace a meal.

Foods with protein, such as low-fat cottage cheese or eggs, may help you feel more satisfied than carbohydrate-rich foods, such as crackers, which are not allowed during this stage anyway.

STAGE 4

DIET: Soft and moist ground or pureed foods

DIETARY GOALS: Drink at least 64 ounces of fluid per day and get a minimum of 50 to 60 grams of protein per day.

INSTRUCTIONS: Most patients begin stage 4 two to four weeks after the gastric band is placed. It usually lasts for 3 to 4 weeks. This stage includes very soft and moist high-protein foods, such as lean ground hamburger, lean ground chicken and turkey, veggie burgers, low-fat cheeses (less than 5 grams per ounce), low-fat chili, fish, and lentils.

Some people may find they still can't tolerate lean ground hamburger, even with low-fat gravy, so they may need pureed meat or chicken. In fact, many band surgeons around the country who do large numbers of gastric banding surgeries keep their patients on liquids for two weeks, then purees for two weeks, and then solids by week four. Check with your surgical center regarding its specific guidelines for advancing your diet after your banding surgery.

However, the vast majority of my patients are able to tolerate ground or very soft foods included in this stage, especially if they add moisture (such as lemon to fish or low-fat gravy to chicken). The big problem foods for many people after banding surgery are steak and chicken, along with doughy breads, rice, and pasta.

My patients typically are started on chewable multivitamins/minerals and chewable calcium with vitamin D at the two-week postop visit, which is when they are almost always advanced to stage 4.

When in stage 4, ensure that you try only one new food at a time. Also, when in doubt, try only a small amount. This will help you to tolerate the diet and decrease your risk for vomiting, which is never a good thing. Persistent vomiting is never normal, and should necessitate a visit with your surgeon for assessment.

Continue to eat slowly, take pencil-eraser-size bites, and chew your food thoroughly. Remember to chew all foods to a liquid consistency and stop eating when you feel full. Mindful eating includes not only eating slowly but also removing distractions during a meal, such as the television or computer. It may take quite a bit of getting used to, but you may find a new-found pleasure in really savoring your meals, and your dining companions may learn how to eat mindfully as well, which is certainly a bonus!

Employing moist cooking methods, such as baking, roasting, steaming, or poaching is preferable to grilling or barbecuing foods. Since fluids are not permitted with meals, or 30 minutes after meals, consuming dry, tough foods, such as grilled steak, may increase your risk of the food getting "stuck" in your chest area and/or may greatly increase the chance you will vomit, which is unpleasant and potentially dangerous.

Foods that are not very well-tolerated in stage 4 include red meat, pasta, doughy breads, rice, dry or tough chicken or turkey, skins of certain vegetables and fruits such as potatoes and apples, and the membranes of citrus fruits.

STAGE 5

DIET: A healthy diet of low-fat, low-sugar solid foods

DIETARY GOALS: Drink at least 64 ounces of fluid per day and get approximately 60 to 80 grams of protein daily.

INSTRUCTIONS: Usually about 5 to 6 weeks after gastric banding surgery, I advance my patients to the fifth and final stage of the postop gastric banding diet, which is a solid, low-fat, low-sugar healthy diet. This is the final stage! It includes fruits, vegetables, and starches, as well as protein foods and dairy, and it is considered an over-all healthy diet.

Please remember to add only one new food at a time. Certain foods you ate your whole life may not go down well now, such as grilled beef. Keeping an accurate food diary may help you to better ascertain which foods are well-tolerated, and which foods may just not be right for you. You can try offending foods again later, but there may be some foods that may just not sit right in your body after your gastric banding surgery. That may be true for a few weeks, or perhaps that food may never settle right in your stomach after your surgery. Because there are so many potential foods you may be able to tolerate well, stick to those rather than continually getting ill by trying to force your body to tolerate a food that just doesn't go down or settle well.

Although banding patients don't experience dumping syndrome from sugars, typi-cally seen with gastric bypass patients, it's important to select lower calorie alterna-tives for weight loss.

As you go through stage 5, always eat and drink mindfully, chewing foods to a liq-uid consistency. Continue avoiding fluids with meals and 30 minutes after meals.

Chewable multivitamin/mineral and calcium supplements with vitamin D are con-tinued daily.

It's always a good idea to keep in close contact with your surgical center, especially after surgery, in order to make certain that you're meeting your nutritional needs, and that everything is going well overall after your gastric banding surgery. Please ensure that you keep all of your appointments with your clinicians, including those with your surgeon for a potential fill or adjustment. Our gastric banding patients are asked to see their surgeon once a month for the first year postop, to confirm that they are doing well, and to evaluate whether they need a fill or adjustment to increase their restriction (increased level of fullness while eating). Our patients typically receive an adjustment to their band if they are feeling continuously hungry, and/or weight loss has stopped or slowed dramatically (or weight has gone up).

Biliopancreatic Diversion, with or without a Duodenal Switch

CONGRATULATIONS ON YOUR BILIOPANCREATIC DIVERSION (BPD), WITH OR WITHOUT A DUODENAL SWITCH SURGERY!

The BPD surgery has two components. The first part of this procedure is a limited gastrectomy—partial removal of up to two-thirds the stomach. This makes people eat less, so they lose weight, especially in the first year after the surgery. The second part of this procedure involves construction of a long limb Roux-en-Y anastamosis. This is a connection that in some cases is similar to that seen in gastric bypass surgery, where the new stomach is connected to the small intestine at a lower level, but has a short common alimentary channel (the part where food travels through) of 50 centimeters in length.

This part of the procedure causes food to pass straight through the body, and not be absorbed by the body, which is key to maintaining long-term weight loss.

Sometimes the BDP surgery is done with a duodenal switch. In this procedure, the pylorus, the common alimentary channel, is 75 to 100 centimeters. This is probably more information than you need to know, but the BPD with the duodenal switch may help improve tolerance to the diet after your surgery, compared to the classic BPD surgery.

Vitamin and Mineral Absorption

The most serious nutritional risk of BPD surgery is malabsorption of protein, vitamins, and minerals. To combat this, people who have undergone BPD surgery need to take extra calcium and vitamins—especially fat-soluble vitamins A, D, E, and K—for the rest of their lives. Vitamin A deficiency causes night blindness. Vitamin D deficiency causes hyperparathyroidism, which leads to premature osteoporosis. Iron deficiency is sometimes seen, which leads to anemia. Other malabsorption problems are linked to low protein (hypoalbuminemia), edema (fluid build-up), and alopecia (hair loss). In light of possibly serious nutritional complications, individuals who have undergone this procedure need to ensure they follow up with their surgical centers for the rest of their lives.

One of the benefits of this surgery is that 75 percent of the fat you eat is discharged through bowel movements as waste. However, about 50 percent of protein is also discharged, which supports the need for at least 80 grams of protein per day. High-protein foods, such as fish, eggs, soft chicken or turkey, and tofu are possible sources in the diet to help meet your higher protein needs. (Please see the sample menu for "later stages" under the gastric bypass diet guideline in this book for a visual of a potential daily menu suggestion for you to follow after this surgery.)

Mealtime Considerations

It is important not to drink liquids with your meals, or approximately 30 minutes after your meals, because it may not only decrease nutrient absorption, but may also keep you from meeting your protein needs, which are higher than those for gastric banding and gastric bypass surgery. Because your stomach may only hold a maximum of 4 to 6 ounces after your BPD surgery, you may feel full after eating only a few tablespoons of food. Even if you're eating slowly and mindfully (pencil-eraser-size bites, chewing 15 times before swallowing, etc.), your stomach typically stretches over time. However, it may take several months, even up to one year, for your new stomach to stabilize, and for you to figure out how much food your body can handle at one sitting.

As with the other weight-loss surgeries, it's important to eat slowly and mindfully. Mindful eating is extremely important, not only for long-term weight loss, but to help decrease the risk of stretching your new stomach, as well as worsening potential issues related to loose stools and gas. Keeping the picture (or actual model!) of a pencil eraser while you're eating your meals should help remind you of the ideal bite size. Also, you should chew each bite at least 15 times, until the food is a liquid consistency.

Because there is more intestinal bypassing in this surgery (more than gastric bypass surgery, for example), you may want to limit high-fat foods, such as fried foods and fatty meats, because they may greatly increase your risk for diarrhea, gas, and a "blah" feeling because fats really delay the emptying of your stomach. Also, the BPD surgery already increases your chances of having frequent loose stools and gas, and high-fat foods will just magnify these issues.

However, some people who have had BPD surgery lose more weight when eating certain higher fat foods (preferably healthy foods, like salmon and other fatty fish) because it fills them up quickly, but only about 25 percent gets absorbed. Conversely, if they eat foods low in fat, and high in carbs, they may gain weight. This weight gain may happen because the overall transit time is much faster with fats among people who have had this surgery.

BPD surgery affects absorption of not only vitamins, but also medications. Many people may not realize the possible issues seen with malabsorption in this surgery, such as excessive loose stools, which may cause issues with low potassium, for example, and can be potentially dangerous because your heart needs a normal potassium level to beat properly. Also, malabsorption after BPD surgery may result in hair loss, skin dryness, and dry and brittle nails. It's important to take all of the vitamins and other supplements, such as calcium with vitamin D, exactly as your surgical center recommends to help lower your risks for nutritional deficiencies.

The Importance of Protein

After your surgery, you will have a goal of how much protein to eat each day. Protein is essential for preserving lean or muscle mass, and it is vital for wound healing, so it's imperative right after surgery that you try to get in at least 60 to 70 grams of protein within the first few weeks of your surgery. Ideally, you'll be able to reach the 100-gram protein mark (about 15 ounces total of chicken, fish, etc.) within a few months of your procedure.

To help guarantee that you meet your protein needs, you should try to include protein in every meal and snack. The latter should not include things like crackers, chips, and other high-carbohydrate foods that may be very well-tolerated but could fill you up, possibly keeping you from getting enough protein, and potentially resulting in weight gain down the road (if you "graze" or eat these snack foods continuously throughout the day). Snacks that I recommend, within the proper diet stage, include low-fat cheeses (less than 3 grams of fat per ounce, ideally); low-fat, low-sugar yogurts; low-fat cottage cheese; fat-free ricotta cheese; and egg whites. People who have undergone the BPD procedure may need as much as 100 grams (about 15 ounces) of protein a day, which is the equivalent of five decks of cards worth of chicken! That's a lot of chicken (or equivalent) in one day, especially if you're not feeling at all hungry after your surgery. Therefore, I often encourage my BPD patients to consume up to six small, high-protein meals per day (such as 1½ ounces chicken at lunch, ½ cup low-fat cottage cheese in between lunch and dinner, 2 ounces of fish at dinner, ½ cup fat-free ricotta cheese at night, etc.).

If adequate protein intake is still a struggle several weeks after surgery, I often recommend a very high-protein, no-carbohydrate, fat-free drink, found in most health food stores. These drinks contain about 40 grams of protein (soy or whey are good quality protein sources to look for) per 20 ounces of liquid supplement, so I recommend splitting it into 8- or 10-ounce glasses, up to 4 times per day (total of 80 grams of protein for 40 ounces) as needed to help meet protein needs while solid high-protein food intake is suboptimal. I don't advise drinking more than 10 ounces (or 20 grams of protein) at one time because protein requires water to flush out the breakdown products, and therefore can be dehydrating, as well as potentially taxing to your kidneys.

Decreased Appetite

A decreased appetite is quite common after BPD, and it is thought to be related to minimization of hunger hormones after this surgery. It's sometimes called the "honeymoon period," and it can last more than a year postoperatively. Believe it or not, you may need to constantly remind yourself to eat for some time after your surgery. This may sound ideal before surgery, but in reality can sometimes feel like a part-time job, at least per some of my BPD patients' comments.

As with the other weight-loss surgeries, it is really important to introduce only one new food at a time. This way, if you feel sick or vomit after you eat it, you'll have a better idea of what the offending food or beverage was.

Avoid Concentrated Sugars

Concentrated sugars, like table sugar (sucrose), should be avoided. They're not only filled with empty calories, but also could result in dumping syndrome, which often manifests as a shaky, sweaty feeling, often leaving people extremely tired. It's best to

Artificial Sweeteners: How Sweet They Are

Artificial sweeteners, also known as sugar substitutes, are designed to replace table sugar (or sucrose) in order to sweeten foods and beverages. You need to use less sugar substitute than sugar because artificial sweeteners are many times sweeter than table sugar. These sweeteners are regulated by the U.S. Food and Drug Administration (FDA).

Here are the most common artificial sweeteners found on the market and some general information regarding their uses:

SPLENDA (SUCRALOSE)

This artificial sweetener was approved by the FDA as a tabletop sweetener in 1998, and then as a general-purpose sweetener in 1999. Splenda is often regarded as "natural" because it's made from real sugar, although it's chemically combined with chlorine, a process most would consider unnatural. Splenda is 600 times sweeter than table sugar. It may be of benefit for people with diabetes, because it has been deemed to have no effect on carbohydrate metabolism, short- or long-term blood sugar control, or insulin secretion.

Splenda is considered to be very stable, so it's a popular ingredient in almost every type of food and beverage, including diet sodas, juice drinks, and teas. However, the biggest selling point is the ability to bake with Splenda, which isn't possible with most of the other artificial sweeteners.

EQUAL AND NUTRASWEET (ASPARTAME)

Aspartame, distributed under the trade names Equal and Nutrasweet, was approved in 1981 by the FDA, and it became the artificial sweetener of choice when saccharin decreased in popularity many years ago. It's derived from the amino acids (building blocks of protein) aspartic acid and phenylalanine. People who have a rare genetic disorder called PKU (phenylketonuria) can't break down phenyalanine, so they must totally avoid aspartame. However, it has been deemed safe for people with diabetes, as it seems to produce a very small rise in blood sugar.

This sweetener is 200 times sweeter than table sugar, and it is often used in beverages, ice cream, and puddings. Aspartame's sweetness is enhanced by other flavors and sweeteners, but it loses its sweetness when heated. Therefore, it is not ideal for baking. However, Sugar Lite, a new product that is a combination of table sugar and aspartame, can be used in baking. One teaspoon of this product contains 8 calories, which is half the calories of a teaspoon of pure table sugar.

SWEET'N LOW AND SUGAR TWIN (SACCHARIN)

Saccharin, which is sold as Sweet'N Low and Sugar Twin, is the oldest of the approved artificial sweeteners. In 1977, the FDA tried to ban saccharin based on research indicating it caused cancer in animals. However, it remained on the shelves, but with a warning regarding this finding. In 2000, the National Institutes of Health (NIH) removed saccharin from its list of cancer-causing agents (carcinogens), and the necessity of including the warning label regarding the animal studies was waived. Although saccharin has been cleared by the FDA, it continues to be a bit controversial.

Like other artificial sweeteners, saccharine produces no sugar (or glycemic) response. It is 300 times sweeter than table sugar, and it is used in many products. Sugar Twin, which is a combination of maltodextrin and sodium saccharin, contains 0 calories per teaspoon, but it measures the same as sugar, cup for cup. However, the label on the box states that Sugar Twin is not appropriate for recipes calling for more than $1/2$ cup of sugar. Therefore, this product is not ideal for baking overall. It may be ideal though, for sweetening coffee or tea.

STEVIA (SWEET LEAF)

This sweetener is considered the ultimate "natural" sweetener, and it has been quite popular lately in the United States. It is extracted from a shrub that grows in South America. Because our bodies can't metabolize sweet leaf or break it down, it does not provide calories. Stevia is approved as a supplement, but not a food. Therefore, you can find it in a pharmacy, but not in a grocery store. It has not yet been approved by the FDA, but it may be in the near future.

SUNETTE (ACESULFAME POTASSIUM)

This artificial sweetener was approved by the FDA in 1988. It is 200 times sweeter than table sugar, and it produces no blood sugar response. It is often found in diet sodas, juice drinks, gums, and ice cream. However, it's not available for use in baking or cooking.

SUGAR ALCOHOLS (SORBITOL, MANNITOL)

For many years, people with diabetes have used products with sugar alcohols—such as sorbitol, mannitol, xylitol, and malitol—to sweeten foods without the sugar or glycemic response seen with table sugar. These are natural sweeteners that do not trigger an insulin reaction. Sugar alcohols contain half the calories of sugar, and they are not digested by the small intestine.

It is important to realize that sorbitol, one of the sugar alcohols commonly found on the market, is a natural laxative, and it may cause diarrhea, bloating, and flatulence. I often tell my patients not to try sugar alcohols for the first time while you're on a camping trip, since the potential laxative effect could be quite embarrassing and uncomfortable. However, for people having constipation issues, sugar-alcohol-sweetened products, in moderation, may help alleviate this problem. It is often found in sugar-free candies, as well as some high-protein bars.

Try these Web sites for more information regarding artificial sweeteners:

Splenda: www.splenda.com

Stevia: www.stevia.com

Sweet'N Low: www.sweetnlow.com

Equal: www.equal.com

Sugar Twin: www.sugartwin.com

Saccharin: www.saccharin.org

The following cookbooks feature artificial sweeteners:

Cooking Healthy with Splenda, by JoAnna M. Lund and Barbara Alpert, Perigee Trade Books, 2004.

Graham Kerr's Simply Splenda Cookbook, by Graham Kerr, American Diabetes Association, 2004.

Unbelievable Desserts with Splenda: Sweet Treats Low in Sugar, Fat and Calories, by Marlene Koch, M. Evans & Company, Inc., 2001.

500 Low-Carb Recipes, by Dana Carpender, Fair Winds Press, 2002.

Protein Powders: What's the Scoop?

Many of my weight-loss surgery patients ask me about protein powders, and it seems there are new ones cropping up almost daily. How do you know which ones are best? Also, are there any possible things to watch out for with some of the protein powders, such as intolerance issues?

Protein powders can vary greatly in terms of quality, and they may be a mixture of two or more different kinds of proteins. In terms of pure sources of protein, there are four general types: whey, soy, egg, and rice. Let's talk about each in turn.

RICE PROTEIN

Rice protein is made by carefully extracting the protein from brown rice. Although rice is often overlooked because of its incomplete amino acids, or building blocks of protein, rice powders are typically supplemented with L-amino acids to make them complete.

Benefits of rice protein: Rice protein is hypoallergenic, so it's ideal for people with soy, milk, or egg allergies or sensitivities. It is also perfect for vegans or strict vegetarians.

WHEY PROTEIN

This is taken from milk, and is the most popular type of protein supplement on the market. Because it is a derivative of milk, it contains some lactose, or milk sugar. People who are lactose intolerant shouldn't take whey protein. Also, because gastric bypass and biliopancreatic diversion patients may have lactose intolerance issues after surgery, whey protein can cause a problem. If you have gas, abdominal bloating, cramping, and/or diarrhea every time you take whey protein, you may be lactose intolerant. Try taking the whey protein along with the enzyme lactase, which you can purchase over the counter at any pharmacy and many supermarkets. When taken with whey protein powder, this enzyme should eliminate the problem by breaking down the milk sugar (lactose) to lactic acid, thereby doing away with the symptoms.

Whey protein powders contain both essential amino acids (building blocks of protein the body cannot make) and nonessential amino acids (building blocks of protein that can be made in the body). Whey is easily taken up and used by the muscles in the body, and it is considered very safe to use.

There are two types of whey protein powders: concentrate and isolate. The concentrate form is more common, easier to find, and less expensive. It contains between 30 and 85 percent protein. Whey isolate is a higher quality protein, so it's more expensive than the concentrate. Because whey isolate contains more than 90 percent protein, it's more easily absorbed by the body, and it also contains less fat and lactose (milk sugar).

Benefits of whey protein: Whey protein may help boost immunity. It is an ideal source of amino acids. It also may help prevent muscle breakdown and speed up muscle recovery after exercise.

SOY PROTEIN

Soy protein comes from soy flour, so it is a good protein source for vegans. Soy is the most complete vegetable protein available. Like whey protein powders, soy protein also has two varieties: concentrate and isolate. The isolate is the more expensive form, because it is more pure and has a higher percentage of protein, compared to the concentrate. Soy protein is typically very easy to digest, and it can be considered as high a quality protein as milk and meat. I often recommend soy protein powders to my weight-loss surgery patients who have a milk allergy or lactose intolerance issues.

Benefits of soy protein: Soy protein is ideal for vegans, and it's perfect for people with milk intolerance or allergies. There are studies suggesting moderate soy consumption may help lower cholesterol and possibly reduce the risk of heart disease, although some recent studies seem to be challenging this claim.

EGG PROTEIN

Egg protein powders are made from egg whites, so they are very high in protein and essentially fat-free. Egg protein is considered a perfect protein, with a grade of 100 in terms of biological value. Egg protein is complete in essential amino acids, and it also has other amino acids, such as branched chain amino acids (leucine, isoleucine, and valine) and glutamic acid. The branched chain amino acids and glutamic acid may be especially useful after weight-loss surgery, because they tend to help muscles recover more quickly. However, egg protein powders should not be used by anyone with an egg allergy.

Benefits of egg protein: Egg protein is fat-free, fairly inexpensive, and not an issue for people with milk or lactose intolerance or soy intolerance or sensitivity.

Lynette's Tips for Stocking an Efficient Kitchen

I can't count the number of times I've heard people say, "If only I could just make a few things turn out right in the kitchen!" Maybe you've uttered the same words. We are so pleased to present this cookbook to you that will guide you step-by-step through producing these user-friendly and delicious recipes and also help you become aware of some basic and essential culinary rules to live by. From cooking for your family, to entertaining, there is something here for everyone. Let's begin with your kitchen. Here are a few good tips to follow to make your culinary adventures easy, fun, and educational.

It's essential to have a few standard pieces of equipment in your kitchen, which will make preparing any meal faster. **A set of good sharp knives** is an absolute must, along with a block to store them in to keep them from becoming dull quickly. A chef's blade (8- to 10-inch, or 20 to 25 cm), a fillet or boning knife, a serrated knife, and a small paring knife will get you through just about any recipe you'll ever prepare.

A pair of ordinary kitchen shears is also a good idea. Shears are wonderful for removing skin and fat from meat and poultry, for trimming vegetables of their stems and other unwanted parts, and for opening stubborn packages.

A set of nonstick pots and pans is a good item to have. Choose one that has thicker-gauged bottoms, which will promote even heat distribution and help to avoid constant scorching. Find the set that looks right for you in your local department store. A 7- or 9-piece set is sufficient to begin with, and then as you become more adventurous you'll soon learn what additional pieces you wish to add to your collection.

Next, **a set of stainless steel mixing bowls** can make your kitchen endeavors easier and more efficient. I prefer stainless steel over glass or plastic because it is light-weight but sturdy enough to handle an electric mixer or being dropped without breaking. In addition to being sturdy, stainless steel holds temperatures more efficiently than plastic or glass, neither of which conducts heat or cold. In other words, the item you are mixing in stainless steel will hold its temperature longer rather than rise or fall to room temperature like it will in glass or plastic. Choose a set of mixing bowls ranging in size from 1 to 5 quarts (1 to 5 liters) to meet all of your mixing needs. When mixing anything in your mixing bowls, be sure to leave plenty of room for the product to be sufficiently manipulated. Always use a bowl that is twice the size of the product you are mixing.

A food processor is essential for preparing purees and certain types of sauces. A blender can be used in place of a food processor. However, a blender may not be sufficient for certain applications, such as finely chopping onions and peppers or grinding meat and other products. Since blenders are essentially designed for liquids, gravity plays an important role in their design. A food processor, however, is designed to expose more surface area of the product being processed by the working blade and so gravity is not such a factor. There are a variety of processors on the market today, and you can buy a decent one at a department store.

It is a good idea to keep **one colander** and **one fine mesh strainer or sieve** in your kitchen. It is important to wash vegetables before preparing them, and these are the tools to use. You will find many other uses for these simple and inexpensive items as well.

Eventually you will learn what works best for your kitchen and your own style as it develops. That's true for kitchen equipment, but also for food. Here are a few of my own essentials items I recommend having on hand at all times.

Ordinary table salt may be easily accessible, although it may not be the best choice for cooking. A **good sea salt** can be found at the grocer, as well as **kosher salt.** A little bit of either of these salts goes a long way.

Fresh cracked or fresh ground pepper can have a great deal more flavor compared to prepackaged ground pepper. Oil in the peppercorn dehydrates at a much faster rate after it is ground, and so the flavor dissipates as well. Truly fresh black pepper will have a fruity aroma and a hearty bite. In addition, I find that it's worth researching where your spices come from. Dried spices and seasonings will lose the intensity of flavor as they age. Quality ingredients, including spices and seasonings, can contribute a world of difference to your recipes.

Lemons are also essential in your kitchen. You will find many recipes in this book that require fresh lemon juice and lemon zest. Zest is the outer portion of the rind that is grated off with a zester or a fine grating surface. The flavor is very intense, and not at all bitter like the inner white portion of the rind. You will also find recipes in this book using fresh lime and orange zest.

There are many **substitutes available for butter,** such as light butters, margarines, and butter alternatives. I recommend reduced-fat and reduced-calorie butter in place of margarine, because of the usually high sodium content in margarine. Some spreads contain olive oil and offer a rich flavor and good heat conduction when using for a sauté. When using a butter alternative or oil to sauté foods, always be sure to thoroughly heat it before adding the ingredients to be sautéed, unless the recipe states otherwise.

Quite a few recipes in the book call for **wine.** If you prefer not to cook using alcohol, any of our recipes calling for the use of wine can be made without compromising flavor or consistency simply by substituting chicken or vegetable broth or water with a bit of lemon juice for the wine.

You'll find that the recipes often offer ranges of time for cooking, such as bake for 20 to 30 minutes, instead of exact numbers. That's because each oven, stovetop, refrigerator, and freezer varies in temperature. Likewise, different pots, pans, and baking dishes will all conduct temperatures to varying degrees, and so it is necessary to make adjustments to cooking time and temperatures as you progress through any recipe.

As you're cooking, to save time and also to stay organized in your kitchen, it's always best to have all of the measured, cut, and prepared ingredients ready to use before you begin the recipe.

Here's an important food safety note. **It's important to keep the work surfaces, such as counter tops and cutting boards, clean and sanitized.** An ordinary kitchen sponge will transfer concentrated amounts of bacteria from every surface it has touched since it was placed into use. One of the best solutions for sanitizing is simply bleach and tap water, in the proportion of one capful of bleach to one gallon of water. If too much bleach is used, the solution will evaporate before it has sufficient time to sanitize. Also, bleach in the solution will evaporate if the temperature of the water is too hot.

Now that you have the basic recommendations for setting up your kitchen, we hope all of your culinary endeavors are delicious, nutritious, exciting, and fun!

CHAPTER 2

Breakfasts and Brunches

All-American Scramble

To save time, prepare the turkey bacon ahead of time per the package instructions. Serve this, or any of the scrambles in this book, with a slice of whole grain toast or English muffin for a complete breakfast. You can leave out the cheese from any of these scrambles.

GBP: Weeks 3–6 Postop

BAND: Weeks 3–6 Postop

BPD: Weeks 2–4 Postop

INGREDIENTS

- 1 teaspoon light butter
- 1 slice turkey bacon, crumbled
- ¼ cup (60 ml) liquid egg substitute
- 1 tablespoon (7 g) reduced-fat shredded Cheddar cheese

In an omelet pan, melt the butter over medium heat, swirling the pan to coat evenly.

Add the turkey bacon and sauté 4 to 5 minutes, until it becomes soft and just begins to brown. Add the egg substitute, stirring gently but constantly with a heat-resistant rubber spatula, scraping the bottom of the pan to keep the eggs moving to avoid browning. When the eggs are almost finished, add the cheese and turn off the heat. Gently fold the cheese into the eggs, turning over with the spatula. When the cheese becomes soft, but not dissolved, turn the scramble onto a plate.

YIELD: Makes 1 serving.

NUTRITIONAL ANALYSIS

Each with: **Calories:** 118.13 **Protein:** 11.03 g **Carbs:** 0.59 g **Total Fat:** 7.89 g **Sat Fat:** 2.09 g **Cholesterol:** 14.38 mg **Sodium:** 379.82 mg **Sugars:** 0.40 g **Fiber:** 0.00 g

Denver Scramble

GBP: Weeks 4–6 Postop

BAND: Weeks 4–6 Postop

BPD: Weeks 2–4 Postop

INGREDIENTS

- 1 teaspoon light butter
- 1^1/$_2$ teaspoons chopped green bell pepper
- 1^1/$_2$ teaspoons chopped yellow onion
- 1^1/$_2$ teaspoons chopped tomato
- 1 slice (1 ounce, or 28 g) reduced-sodium, reduced-fat ham, chopped
- ^{1}/$_4$ cup (60 ml) liquid egg substitute
- 1 tablespoon (7 g) reduced-fat shredded Cheddar cheese

In an omelet pan over medium heat, melt the butter, swirling the pan to coat evenly.

Add the pepper, onion, and tomato and cook 4 to 5 minutes, until they become soft. Add the ham and continue cooking, until heated through. Add the egg substitute, stirring gently but constantly with a heat-resistant rubber spatula, scraping the bottom of the pan to keep the eggs moving to avoid browning. When the eggs are almost finished, add the cheese and turn off the heat. Gently fold the cheese into the eggs, turning over with the spatula. When the cheese becomes soft but not dissolved, turn the scramble onto a plate.

YIELD: Makes 1 serving.

NUTRITIONAL ANALYSIS

Each with: **Calories:** 126.55 **Protein:** 13.96 g **Carbs:** 3.48 g **Total Fat:** 6.34 g **Sat Fat:** 1.60 g **Cholesterol:** 17.38 mg **Sodium:** 381.03 mg **Sugars:** 1.15 g **Fiber:** 0.39 g

Ground Beef and Spinach Scramble

GBP: Weeks 4-6 Postop

BAND: Weeks 4-6 Postop

BPD: Weeks 2-4 Postop

INGREDIENTS

- 1 teaspoon light butter
- 6 teaspoons lean, browned ground beef
- $1/3$ cup (10 g) chopped fresh spinach leaves, stems removed
- $1/4$ cup (60 ml) liquid egg substitute
- 1 tablespoon (5 g) shredded Parmesan cheese

In an omelet pan over medium heat, melt the butter, swirling the pan to coat evenly. Add the ground beef and sauté 4 to 5 minutes, until warmed through. Add the spinach and continue cooking, until the spinach is completely wilted. Add the egg substitute, stirring gently but constantly with a heat-resistant rubber spatula, scraping the bottom of the pan to keep the eggs moving to avoid browning. When the eggs are almost finished, add the cheese and turn off the heat. Gently fold the cheese into the eggs, turning over with the rubber spatula. When the cheese becomes soft but not dissolved, turn the scramble onto a plate.

YIELD: Makes 1 serving.

NUTRITIONAL ANALYSIS

Each with: **Calories:** 141.75 **Protein:** 17.45 g **Carbs:** 0.93 g **Total Fat:** 7.29 g **Sat Fat:** 2.47 g **Cholesterol:** 24.92 mg **Sodium:** 250.21 mg **Sugars:** 0.61 g **Fiber:** 0.22 g

Mushroom and Swiss Cheese Scramble

GBP: Weeks 4-6 Postop

BAND: Weeks 4-6 Postop

BPD: Weeks 2-4 Postop

INGREDIENTS

- 1 teaspoon light butter
- $1/4$ cup (15 g) sliced mushrooms
- $1/4$ cup (60 ml) liquid egg substitute
- 1 slice (1 ounce, or 28 g) low-fat Swiss cheese, cut into strips

In an omelet pan over medium heat, melt the butter, swirling the pan to coat evenly.

Add the mushrooms and sauté about 4 to 5 minutes, until they become soft and just begin to brown. Add the egg substitute, stirring gently but constantly with a heat-resistant rubber spatula, scraping the bottom of the pan to keep the eggs moving to avoid browning. When the eggs are almost finished, add the cheese and turn off the heat. Gently fold the cheese into the eggs, turning over with the rubber spatula. When the cheese becomes soft but not dissolved, turn the scramble onto a plate.

YIELD: Makes 1 serving.

NUTRITIONAL ANALYSIS

Each with: **Calories:** 171.85 **Protein:** 19.29 g **Carbs:** 2.24 g **Total Fat:** 9.27 g **Sat Fat:** 3.57 g **Cholesterol:** 17.63 mg **Sodium:** 223.34 mg **Sugars:** 1.46 g **Fiber:** 0.68 g

Greek Scramble

GBP: Weeks 4-6 Postop

BAND: Weeks 4-6 Postop

BPD: Weeks 2-4 Postop

INGREDIENTS

- 1 teaspoon light butter
- $1/2$ teaspoon chopped fresh thyme leaves
- $1/4$ cup (60 ml) liquid egg substitute
- 2 large pitted black olives, sliced
- 2 teaspoons finely-diced green bell pepper
- 2 teaspoons feta cheese crumbles

In an omelet pan over medium heat, melt the butter, swirling the pan to coat evenly. Add the thyme and sauté about 1 to 2 minutes, until it begins to bubble and sweat. Add the egg substitute, stirring gently but constantly with a heat-resistant rubber spatula, scraping the bottom of the pan to keep the eggs moving to avoid browning. When the eggs are almost finished, add the olives, pepper, and cheese and turn off the heat. Gently fold the ingredients into the eggs, turning over with the rubber spatula. When the cheese becomes soft but not dissolved, turn the scramble onto a plate.

YIELD: Makes 1 serving.

NUTRITIONAL ANALYSIS

Each with: **Calories:** 96.95 **Protein:** 8.61 g **Carbs:** 1.78 g **Total Fat:** 5.97 g **Sat Fat:** 1.68 g **Cholesterol:** 6.19 mg **Sodium:** 247.13 mg **Sugars:** 1.42 g **Fiber:** 0.38 g

Tomato and Fresh Basil Scramble

GBP: Weeks 4–6 Postop

BAND: Weeks 4–6 Postop

BPD: Weeks 2–4 Postop

INGREDIENTS

- 1 teaspoon light butter
- 2 tablespoons (20 g) chopped tomato
- 1½ teaspoons chopped fresh basil leaves
- ¼ cup (60 ml) liquid egg substitute
- 1 tablespoon (5 g) shredded Parmesan cheese

In an omelet pan over medium heat, melt the butter, swirling the pan to coat evenly. Add the tomato and continue cooking 4 to 5 minutes, until soft. Add the basil and egg substitute, stirring gently but constantly with a heat-resistant rubber spatula, scraping the bottom of the pan to keep the eggs moving to avoid browning. When the eggs are almost finished, add the cheese and turn off the heat. Gently fold the cheese into the eggs, turning over with the spatula. When the cheese becomes soft but not dissolved, turn the scramble onto a plate.

YIELD: Makes 1 serving.

NUTRITIONAL ANALYSIS

Each with: **Calories:** 98.72 **Protein:** 9.82 g **Carbs:** 2.53 g **Total Fat:** 5.58 g **Sat Fat:** 1.63 g **Cholesterol:** 4.23 mg **Sodium:** 228.78 mg **Sugars:** 1.38 g **Fiber:** 0.74 g

Zucchini, Bacon, and Swiss Cheese Scramble

To save time, prepare the turkey bacon ahead of time per the package instructions.

GBP: Weeks 4–6 Postop

BAND: Weeks 4–6 Postop

BPD: Weeks 2–4 Postop

INGREDIENTS

- 1 teaspoon light butter
- 1 tablespoon (5 g) turkey bacon crumbles
- ¼ cup (30 g) chopped spring zucchini
- ¼ cup (60 ml) liquid egg substitute
- 1 slice (1 ounce, or 28 g) low-fat Swiss cheese, cut into strips

In an omelet pan over medium heat, melt the butter, swirling the pan to coat evenly. Add the bacon and continue cooking 4 to 5 minutes, until heated through. Add the zucchini and cook, until soft. Add the egg substitute, stirring gently but constantly with a heat-resistant rubber spatula, scraping the bottom of the pan to keep the eggs moving to avoid browning. When the eggs are almost finished, add the cheese and turn off the heat. Gently fold the cheese into the eggs, turning over with the spatula. When the cheese becomes soft but not dissolved, turn the scramble onto a plate.

YIELD: Makes 1 serving.

NUTRITIONAL ANALYSIS

Each with: **Calories:** 179.08 **Protein:** 18.88 g **Carbs:** 1.35 g **Total Fat:** 10.39 g **Sat Fat:** 3.81 g **Cholesterol:** 22.69 mg **Sodium:** 320.08 mg **Sugars:** 0.89 g **Fiber:** 0.31 g

Fresh Herb and Goat Cheese Scramble

GBP: Weeks 4–6 Postop

BAND: Weeks 4–6 Postop

BPD: Weeks 2–4 Postop

INGREDIENTS

- 1 teaspoon light butter
- 1 teaspoon chopped fresh parsley
- 1 teaspoon chopped fresh chives
- 1 teaspoon chopped fresh tarragon
- 1/4 cup (60 ml) liquid egg substitute
- 2 teaspoons goat cheese crumbles

In an omelet pan over medium heat, melt the butter, swirling the pan to coat evenly.

Add the parsley, chives, and tarragon and sauté 1 to 2 minutes, until they begin to bubble and sweat. Add the egg substitute, stirring gently but constantly with a heat-resistant rubber spatula, scraping the bottom of the pan to keep the eggs moving to avoid browning. When the eggs are almost finished, add the cheese and turn off the heat. Gently fold the cheese into the eggs, turning over with the spatula. When the cheese becomes soft but not dissolved, turn the scramble onto a plate.

YIELD: Makes 1 serving.

NUTRITIONAL ANALYSIS

Each with: **Calories:** 103.94 **Protein:** 9.90 g **Carbs:** 0.98 g **Total Fat:** 6.66 g **Sat Fat:** 2.51 g **Cholesterol:** 8.07 mg **Sodium:** 166.70 mg **Sugars:** 0.58 g **Fiber:** 0.11 g

Italian Scramble

GBP: Weeks 4–6 Postop

BAND: Weeks 4–6 Postop

BPD: Weeks 2–4 Postop

INGREDIENTS

- 1 teaspoon light butter
- 1/8 teaspoon dried oregano
- 2 teaspoons finely chopped yellow onion
- 1 tablespoon (10 g) chopped tomato
- 1/4 cup (60 ml) liquid egg substitute
- 1 slice (1 ounce, or 28 g) part skim mozzarella, cut into strips

In an omelet pan over medium heat, melt the butter, swirling the pan to coat evenly. Add the oregano and sauté 4 to 5 minutes, until it begins to sweat. Add the onions and continue cooking, until they become soft. Add the tomato and stir just enough to evenly distribute. Add the egg substitute, stirring gently but constantly with a heat-resistant rubber spatula, scraping the bottom of the pan to keep the eggs moving to avoid browning. When the eggs are almost finished, add the cheese and turn off the heat. Gently fold the cheese into the eggs, turning over with the spatula. When the cheese becomes soft but not dissolved, turn the scramble onto a plate.

YIELD: Makes 1 serving.

NUTRITIONAL ANALYSIS

Each with: **Calories:** 158.21 **Protein:** 15.05 g **Carbs:** 1.86 g **Total Fat:** 9.63 g **Sat Fat:** 4.41 g **Cholesterol:** 18.92 mg **Sodium:** 343.86 mg **Sugars:** 1.08 g **Fiber:** 0.27 g

Mark's Fruity French Toast

Mark is a gastric bypass surgery patient in the Boston area who makes this recipe for himself almost every morning and loves it.

GBP: Weeks 6–8 Postop

BAND: Weeks 6–8 Postop

BPD: Weeks 4–6 Postop

INGREDIENTS

- $1/4$ cup (60 ml) liquid egg substitute
- 1 tablespoon (14 ml) nonfat milk
- $1/2$ teaspoon allspice
- 2 slices reduced-calorie whole-wheat bread
- $1/4$ cup (40 g) sliced fresh strawberries
- $1/3$ cup (50 g) fresh blueberries
- $1/8$ cup (30 ml) sugar-free maple syrup

Coat a medium (big enough to hold two slices of bread) nonstick pan with cooking spray.

In a small mixing bowl combine the egg substitute, milk, and allspice. Dip the bread into the egg batter to coat both sides.

Heat the pan over medium heat. Place the bread into the pan and cook on both sides, until golden brown. Transfer the French toast to a serving plate and top with the strawberries, blueberries, and maple syrup.

YIELD: Makes 1 (2-slice) serving.

NUTRITIONAL ANALYSIS
Each with: **Calories:** 221.36 **Protein:** 12.91 g **Carbs:** 39.31 g **Total Fat:** 3.52 g **Sat Fat:** 0.63 g **Cholesterol:** 0.93 mg **Sodium:** 408.18 mg **Sugars:** 9.14 g **Fiber:** 7.65 g

Cumin Mushroom Omelet

This is simple and delicious! For a complete breakfast, serve this delicious omelet with a whole-wheat English muffin half and fresh fruit. Serve it with Fresh Salsa Caliente (page 132).

GBP: Weeks 4–6 Postop

BAND: Weeks 4–6 Postop

BPD: Weeks 2–4 Postop

INGREDIENTS

- $^1/_2$ pound (225 g) mushrooms
- 1 tablespoon (14 g) low-fat butter alternative
- 1 teaspoon olive oil
- 1 small clove garlic, minced
- 2 teaspoons ground cumin
- $^1/_8$ teaspoon cayenne pepper (optional)
- $^1/_4$ teaspoon paprika
- $^1/_4$ teaspoon kosher salt or sea salt
- 2 tablespoons (25 g) nonfat sour cream
- 1 cup (235 ml) liquid egg substitute
- $^3/_4$ cup (85 g) reduced-fat shredded Cheddar cheese
- $^1/_4$ cup (4 g) chopped fresh cilantro
- Fresh cilantro sprigs

Clean the mushrooms with a mushroom brush or paper towels. Cut the end of the stems away and discard. Slice the mushrooms into thin slices.

In a medium nonstick skillet, heat the butter alternative and oil over medium heat. Add the mushrooms, garlic, cumin, pepper, paprika, and salt. Sauté, stirring often, for about 8 minutes, until the mushrooms become soft. Stir in the sour cream and continue cooking for 2 minutes, stirring once or twice. Remove the pan from the heat.

Coat a 7-inch (17.5 cm) nonstick skillet with cooking spray and heat to medium. Add the egg substitute and cook until the bottom becomes solid, but not browned. Using a rubber spatula, carefully lift the sides of the omelet up to let the egg substitute spill underneath the cooked, solid bottom. Repeat this process until the egg mixture is entirely cooked, then turn off the heat. Add the cheese and cilantro to the bottom half of the omelet. Fold the top half over the bottom half and gently press down with the rubber spatula. Cut the omelet in half and slide the halves onto serving plates. Garnish with the cilantro sprigs and salsa.

YIELD: Makes 4 (about $^1/_2$-cup) servings.

NUTRITIONAL ANALYSIS

Each with: **Calories:** 160.93 **Protein:** 14.59 g **Carbs:** 5.09 g **Total Fat:** 9.11 g **Sat Fat:** 3.39 g **Cholesterol:** 13.13 mg **Sodium:** 408.90 mg **Sugars:** 1.99 g **Fiber:** 1.19 g

Berry Delicious Cream of Wheat

GBP: Weeks 4–6 Postop

BAND: Weeks 4–6 Postop

BPD: Weeks 2–4 Postop

INGREDIENTS

- $^3/_4$ cup (135 g) instant Cream of Wheat, no salt added
- $^1/_2$ teaspoon vanilla extract
- $^1/_2$ cup (60 g) fresh raspberries
- 2 tablespoons (15 g) protein powder supplement (see note)
- 2 tablespoons (28 ml) nonfat milk or low-fat, low-sugar soy milk
- 2 sprigs spearmint

Prepare Cream of Wheat per the package instruction for 2 servings, adding the vanilla to the water before boiling. Just before removing the Cream of Wheat from the pan, stir in the raspberries. Add the protein powder just prior to serving. Serve in warmed bowls, topped with the milk and garnished with fresh spearmint sprigs.

YIELD: Makes 2 servings.

"Very satisfying and filling."

—Julie,
a gastric bypass surgery patient in the Boston area

NUTRITIONAL ANALYSIS
Each with: **Calories:** 219.29 **Protein:** 24.88 g **Carbs:** 23.10 g **Total Fat:** 3.21 g **Sat Fat:** 0.07 g **Cholesterol:** 0.28 mg **Sodium:** 83.74 mg **Sugars:** 4.04 **Fiber:** 4.36 g

MARGARET'S NOTES

Although raspberries contain the highest fiber of all berries, you may substitute blueberries, blackberries, strawberries, or huckleberries.

It is essential to select a protein powder that is appropriate for hot foods and beverages for this recipe to optimize the quality of the protein (avoid protein breakdown) when exposed to heat, a process known as denaturing. This is also why you add the protein powder after heating the Cream of Wheat, just prior to serving it.

Berry-Mango Breakfast Shake

This is a great shake to share with friends before a Saturday morning walk. Add a scoop of whey or soy protein powder to this shake for more protein. It's yummy and helps meet your protein needs.

GBP: Weeks 2–4 Postop

BAND: Weeks 2–4 Postop

BPD: Weeks 2–4 Postop

INGREDIENTS

- 1¹⁄₂ cups (385 g) frozen berries (see note)
- 1 cup (165 g) fresh or canned mango slices, chilled
- 1 cup (240 g) soft, silken, low-fat tofu
- 1 cup (235 ml) diet cranberry juice cocktail
- ¹⁄₂ teaspoon vanilla extract
- 6 teaspoons sugar substitute
- 4 sprigs mint

In a blender, process the berries, mango, tofu, juice, vanilla, and sugar substitute, until consistency is smooth. Pour into glasses and top with the mint.

YIELD: Makes 4 (1-cup) servings.

NUTRITIONAL ANALYSIS

Each with: **Calories:** 103.60 **Protein:** 3.52 g **Carbs:** 19.27 g **Total Fat:** 2.13 g **Sat Fat:** 0.05 g **Cholesterol:** 0.00 mg **Sodium:** 6.75 mg **Sugars:** 13.44 g **Fiber:** 4.69 g

NOTE

If you should avoid seeds, choose blueberries.

Greek High-Protein Berry-Licious Milkshake

Delicious Greek yogurt makes this creamy and super nutritious. If you've recently had your weight-loss surgery and can't seem to get solid food in, you could make this shake and have 1 serving (about 1 cup) three times a day for your 3 meals. (Just place the rest in your refrigerator for later use). It will provide more than 60 grams of protein for the 3 servings, which should meet your basic protein needs. The fiber in the berries may help with any constipation problems, which are quite common, especially within the first month or two of weight loss surgery.

GBP: Weeks 2–4 Postop

BAND: Weeks 2–4 Postop

BPD: Weeks 2–4 Postop

INGREDIENTS

- 1 cup (235 ml) nonfat milk or low-fat, low-sugar soy milk (see note)
- 1 cup (150 g) fresh or frozen blueberries, raspberries, strawberries, or blackberries
- 2 ounces (55 g) protein powder supplement
- 7 ounces (200 g) Greek yogurt (2% fat)
- 1 tablespoon (14 ml) sugar-free vanilla syrup
- 1 cup (150 g) crushed ice (optional) (see Lynette's note)

"Yummy and creamy…I used frozen blueberries instead of ice, and it worked great. I used Stevia to sweeten it even more."

—Julie,
a gastric bypass surgery patient in the Boston area

In a blender, combine the milk, blueberries, protein powder, yogurt, syrup, and ice (if using). Blend until the ingredients are emulsified. (The milkshake will be a creamy consistency and blue color throughout.)

YIELD: Makes 3 (about 1-cup) servings.

NUTRITIONAL ANALYSIS

Each with: **Calories:** 179.65 **Protein:** 23.13 g **Carbs:** 15.55 g **Total Fat:** 3.36 g **Sat Fat:** 1.11 g **Cholesterol:** 4.97 mg **Sodium:** 107.57 mg **Sugars:** 11.53 g **Fiber:** 1.16 g

LYNETTE'S NOTE

Add ice cubes to make the shake thicker. But if you add ice cubes, the shake will not hold in the refrigerator.

MARGARET'S NOTE

Make sure the soy milk contains no more than 14 grams of sugar per cup.

Frozen Fruit Smoothie

Frozen fruit smoothies can become a high-protein, easy-to-digest meal when you're on the go, or in the earlier stages of your post-operative diet. You can incorporate them into your diet up to twice a day if you're very busy or if you find your weight is inching upward and you'd like to reverse the trend. If you freeze the bananas for a few hours before making this shake, it will be even thicker and more delicious.

GBP: Weeks 2–4 Postop

BAND: Weeks 2–4 Postop

BPD: Weeks 2–4 Postop

INGREDIENTS

- 4 ounces (115 g) banana, sliced (approximately 8- to 8⁷⁄₈-inches long)
- 1 cup (150 g) fresh or frozen blueberries (see note)
- 1 cup (235 ml) soy milk, unsweetened (see note), or 1 to 1¹⁄₂ cups (235 ml) nonfat milk
- 2 ounces (55 g) protein powder supplement (see note)
- 2 sprigs mint

In a blender, combine the bananas, blueberries, soy milk, and protein powder. Blend for 10 to 15 seconds, until a smooth consistency is reached. Garnish with the mint.

YIELD: Makes 2 servings.

NUTRITIONAL ANALYSIS

Each with: **Calories:** 250.73 **Protein:** 27.09 g **Carbs:** 26.33 g **Total Fat:** 5.01 g **Sat Fat:** 0.06 g **Cholesterol:** 0.00 mg **Sodium:** 85.00 mg **Sugars:** 13.93 g **Fiber:** 5.47 g

"I love this smoothie. I never liked the protein shakes, and I found that I could tolerate the protein in this recipe. In fact, my 3-year-old son loves it too, and we call it "fruit milk." Definitely freeze the bananas. It makes a tasty treat that has some nice chunks in it. I have tried this with blueberries and strawberries in it together, and it is delicious. This is great if you have no time and really want something yummy."

—Julie, *a gastric bypass patient in the New Bedford, Massachusetts, area*

MARGARET'S NOTE

You may substitute raspberries, strawberries, or blackberries for the blueberries, because the calories and carbohydrates are equivalent. Raspberries are the highest in fiber among these fruits, but all contain healthy antioxidants, which are wonderful, cancer-fighting agents.

NOTES

Make sure the soy milk contains no more than 14 grams of sugars per cup.

Generic (low-sugar) protein powders are fine, but please ensure they're appropriate for cold beverages.

Savory Broccoli and Cheese Bread Pudding

This is an elegant breakfast, lunch, or dinner.

GBP: Weeks 6–8 Postop

BAND: Weeks 6–8 Postop

BPD: Weeks 6–8 Postop

INGREDIENTS

- 2 teaspoons olive oil
- 1 medium sweet onion, diced (about 1^1/$_2$ cups, or 240 g)
- ^{1}/$_2$ teaspoon dried oregano
- ^{1}/$_2$ teaspoon dried basil
- ^{1}/$_4$ teaspoon granulated garlic
- 5–6 whole-wheat English muffins, toasted and cut into ^{1}/$_2$-inch (1.25-cm) croutons
- 1 package (14 ounces, or 400 g) chopped frozen broccoli, thawed and drained
- 1^1/$_2$ cups (170 g) reduced-fat shredded Cheddar cheese
- 2 tablespoons (10 g) shredded Parmesan cheese
- 3 large eggs, beaten
- 2 tablespoons (8 g) chopped fresh parsley
- ^{1}/$_2$ cup (120 ml) nonfat half-and-half

Preheat the oven to 350°F (180°C, or gas mark 4).

In a medium skillet, heat the oil over medium-high heat. Add the onion and sauté until it begins to soften. Add the oregano, basil, and garlic and continue cooking for an additional 2 minutes, stirring once or twice. Remove the mixture from heat and set aside.

Coat a 7- x 9-inch (17.5- x 22.5-cm) baking dish with cooking spray. Place the croutons and broccoli in the baking dish. Evenly distribute the sauté mixture over the bread and broccoli. Sprinkle the Cheddar and Parmesan over the croutons and broccoli.

In a small (1 quart, or 1 L) mixing bowl, combine the eggs, parsley, and half-and-half, then pour the egg mixture evenly over the cheese. Bake for 35 minutes, until the center of the dish has risen to meet the level at the edges and the top is golden brown.

YIELD: Makes 12 (^{2}/$_3$-cup) servings.

NUTRITIONAL ANALYSIS

Each with: **Calories:** 196.14 **Protein:** 11.01 g **Carbs:** 25.80 g **Total Fat:** 6.36 g **Sat Fat:** 2.70 g **Cholesterol:** 68.50 mg **Sodium:** 480.27 mg **Sugars:** 6.13 g **Fiber:** 4.49 g

Breakfast Turkey Sausage Patties

Serve these breakfast sausages with any of our egg dishes, frittatas, or egg scrambles and whole-wheat English muffins for a satisfying breakfast or brunch.

GBP: Weeks 6–8 Postop

BAND: Weeks 6–8 Postop

BPD: Weeks 6–8 Postop

INGREDIENTS

- 1 pound (455 g) lean ground turkey (93% fat-free or leaner)
- 1/4 cup (25 g) fine, plain bread crumbs
- 2 teaspoons ground sage
- 1 teaspoon ground coriander
- 1 teaspoon ground oregano
- 1/2 teaspoon ground thyme
- 1/2 teaspoon black pepper
- 1/4 teaspoon sea salt or kosher salt
- 1/4 teaspoon cayenne pepper (optional)
- 1/2 teaspoon paprika
- 1/2 teaspoon garlic powder
- 1/2 cup (120 ml) low-sodium chicken broth

In a large (4 quart, or 4 L) mixing bowl, combine the turkey, bread crumbs, sage, coriander, oregano, thyme, black pepper, salt, cayenne pepper (if using), paprika, and garlic powder. Stir to incorporate completely. Add the broth, stir again, and let stand in the refrigerator for about 20 minutes. Form the mixture into 8 patties, about 1/2-inch (1.25 cm) thick.

Coat a nonstick skillet with cooking spray and heat over medium-high. Cook the patties for about 7 minutes on each side, until browned and done in the center.

YIELD: Makes 8 (about 2-ounce) patties.

NUTRITIONAL ANALYSIS
Each with: **Calories:** 78.73 **Protein:** 14.25 g **Carbs:** 3.32 g **Total Fat:** 1.06 g **Sat Fat:** 0.32 g **Cholesterol:** 27.54 mg **Sodium:** 166.32 mg **Sugars:** 0.27 g **Fiber:** 0.49 g

Zucchini Frittata with Capers and Olives

This is great served with the Chive-Yogurt Sauce below.

GBP: Weeks 6–8 Postop

BAND: Weeks 6–8 Postop

BPD: Weeks 6–8 Postop

INGREDIENTS

- 2 teaspoons extra-virgin olive oil
- 2 cloves garlic, minced
- $1/2$ cup (70 g) finely diced red bell pepper
- 1 cup (160 g) finely diced yellow onion
- 2 cups (250 g) grated zucchini
- 2 tablespoons (20 g) capers, drained
- $1/4$ cup (35 g) finely diced, pitted black or Greek olives
- $1/2$ cup (75 g) feta cheese crumbles
- 2 tablespoons (8 g) chopped fresh parsley
- $2^1/2$ cups (590 ml) liquid egg substitute

Preheat the oven to 375°F (190°C, or gas mark 5). Spray cooking spray around the inside edges of an 8-inch (20-cm) cast iron skillet. In the skillet, heat the oil over medium-high, stirring occasionally. Sauté the garlic, bell pepper, and onion for about 5 minutes, until soft but not brown. Remove the skillet from heat and add the zucchini, capers, and olives. Arrange the cheese and parsley evenly over the sauté mixture. Slowly pour the egg substitute over the top of the mixture in the skillet.

Place the skillet in the oven and bake for 40 minutes, until the center of the frittata rises to match the outer edges. (The frittata should be just beginning to brown when it's finished cooking. If it begins to brown too quickly, reduce the oven temperature to 350°F, 180°C, or gas mark 4.) Serve on warmed plates with Chive-Yogurt Sauce drizzled over the top of each slice.

YIELD: Makes 6 ($1/2$-cup) servings.

NUTRITIONAL ANALYSIS
Each with: **Calories:** 172.69 **Protein:** 15.32 g **Carbs:** 7.03 g **Total Fat:** 8.86 g **Sat Fat:** 2.80 g **Cholesterol:** 12.17 mg **Sodium:** 506.49 mg **Sugars:** 4.01 g **Fiber:** 1.25 g

Chive-Yogurt Sauce

GBP: Weeks 2–4 Postop

BAND: Weeks 2–4 Postop

BPD: Weeks 2–4 Postop

INGREDIENTS

- $1/4$ cup (50 g) nonfat sour cream
- $1/4$ cup (60 g) nonfat plain yogurt
- $1/2$ teaspoon salt
- $1/8$ teaspoon ground white pepper
- 1 tablespoon finely chopped chives

In a small mixing bowl, combine the sour cream, yogurt, salt, pepper, and chives. Vigorously mix with a fork or wire whip.

YIELD: Makes 6 (1-tablespoon) servings

NUTRITIONAL ANALYSIS
Each with: **Calories:** 16.13 **Protein:** 1.06 g **Carbs:** 2.68 g **Total Fat:** 0 g **Sat Fat:** 0 g **Cholesterol:** 1.88 mg **Sodium:** 110.43 mg **Sugars:** 1.30 g **Fiber:** 0.03 g

MARGARET'S NOTE

If you'd like to pack even more protein into this dish, sprinkle part-skim shredded mozzarella cheese or shredded vegetarian (soy) cheese over your frittata, then melt under the broiler until bubbly and golden brown.

Zucchini and Potato Strata

If you like omelets, you'll love this dish. This is a fantastic brunch-style main course that can be prepared the night before and refrigerated. Be sure to bring it just to room temperature before placing it in the oven to avoid cracking the dish.

GBP: Weeks 6–8 Postop

BAND: Weeks 6–8 Postop

BPD: Weeks 6–8 Postop

INGREDIENTS

- 3/4 pounds (340 g) Yukon gold potatoes
- 1 1/2 cups (355 ml) liquid egg substitute
- 2/3 cup (150 ml) nonfat half-and-half
- 1/4 cup (15 g) chopped fresh parsley
- 1/8 teaspoon granulated garlic
- 1/4 teaspoon salt
- 1/8 teaspoon black pepper
- 2 cups (240 g) zucchini slices (cut into thin circles)
- 1 cup (40 g) seasoned croutons
- 1/2 cup (75 g) feta cheese crumbles
- Sprigs fresh parsley

LYNETTE'S NOTES

A lovely topping of warm Pomodoro Sauce (page 222) makes this wonderful dish unforgettable! (3 tablespoons each)

Wash, drain, and peel the potatoes. Using a mandolin slicer or a large chefs knife, slice the potatoes approximately 1/8-inch (3-mm) thick. Place the potatoes into a medium saucepan and cover them with cold water to 1 inch (2.5 cm) above the level of the potatoes. Bring the potatoes just to a boil, then immediately drain them in a colander. Rinse the potatoes in cold water to stop the cooking process and let stand to continue draining.

In a medium mixing bowl, combine the egg substitute, half-and-half, chopped parsley, garlic, salt, and pepper, then whisk together with a wire whip or hand-held blender.

Coat a 9- x 13-inch (22.5- x 32.5-cm) baking dish with cooking spray. Arrange the potatoes in a single layer. Arrange the zucchini on top of the potatoes. Evenly distribute the croutons over the zucchini. Evenly distribute the cheese over the croutons. Pour the egg mixture evenly over top and let stand in the refrigerator for 20 minutes, until the croutons have softened by absorbing the egg mixture.

Preheat the oven to 375°F (190°C, or gas mark 5). Bake the strata for 40 minutes, until the egg mixture is done in the center of the dish and the top is golden brown. Garnish with the parsley sprigs and serve warm.

YIELD: Makes 10 (1-cup) servings.

NUTRITIONAL ANALYSIS
Each with: **Calories:** 192.79 **Protein:** 19.46 g **Carbs:** 11.51 g **Total Fat:** 7.23 g **Sat Fat:** 2.40 g **Cholesterol:** 9.14 mg **Sodium:** 440.91 mg **Sugars:** 3.36 g **Fiber:** 1.08 g

Spring Herb and Zucchini Muffins

Muffins are not your typical post-weight-loss surgery food, but many of my gastric bypass and Band patients tell me they can tolerate them if they're not doughy. I usually don't encourage muffins from a calorie and nutrition perspective, but Lynette concocted some healthy, non-doughy muffins that are as tasty as they are nutritious. Serve these muffins for an elegant accompaniment to a festive and special brunch.

GBP: Weeks 6–8 Postop

BAND: Weeks 6–8 Postop

BPD: Weeks 6–8 Postop

INGREDIENTS

- 1 cup (110 g) all-purpose flour
- $^1/_2$ cup (55 g) oat bran flour
- 1 teaspoon baking powder
- 1 teaspoon baking soda
- $^1/_2$ teaspoon salt
- 1 egg
- 1 tablespoon (14 ml) vegetable oil
- 1 cup (240 g) nonfat plain or vanilla yogurt
- $^3/_4$ cup (95 g) grated zucchini (press out the moisture by squeezing it in paper towels)
- $^1/_4$ cup (60 g) unsweetened applesauce
- 1 tablespoon (3 g) chopped chives
- 1 tablespoon (4 g) chopped fresh parsley
- $1^1/_2$ teaspoons chopped fresh tarragon

Preheat the oven to 375°F (190°C, or gas mark 5). Spray a muffin tin with cooking spray. In a large mixing bowl, combine the all-purpose flour, oat bran flour, baking powder, baking soda, and salt. Stir to combine.

In medium mixing bowl, whisk together the egg, oil, yogurt, zucchini, applesauce, chives, parsley, and tarragon, just enough to combine. (The batter should be slightly lumpy.)

Fill the muffin cups two-thirds full with batter. Bake for 20 to 25 minutes, until a toothpick inserted into the middle of a muffin comes out clean. Let the muffins cool for 15 minutes before turning the tin over to release the muffins. (If the muffins stick to the pan, a slight tap on the back should help to release them.)

YIELD: Makes 12 (2-ounce) muffins.

NUTRITIONAL ANALYSIS

Each with: **Calories:** 85.22 **Protein:** 3.03 g **Carbs:** 14.21 g **Total Fat:** 1.87 g **Sat Fat:** 0.23 g **Cholesterol:** 20.42 mg **Sodium:** 206.11 mg **Sugars:** 2.05 g **Fiber:** 0.92 g

Lavender-Blueberry Muffins

Enjoy the delicious and delightful combination of lavender and blueberries.

GBP: Weeks 6-8 Postop

BAND: Weeks 6-8 Postop

BPD: Weeks 6-8 Postop

INGREDIENTS

- $^1/_3$ cup (65 g) sugar or $^1/_3$ cup (9 g) baking sugar substitute (see page 38) (see Margaret's Note)
- 1 cup (110 g) oat bran flour
- $^1/_2$ cup (55 g) all-purpose flour
- 1 teaspoon baking powder
- 1 teaspoon baking soda
- $^1/_2$ teaspoon salt
- $^1/_4$ cup (60 g) dried lavender (no stems)
- 1 egg
- 1 tablespoon (14 ml) vegetable oil
- 1$^1/_2$ teaspoons vanilla extract
- 1 cup (240 g) nonfat plain or vanilla yogurt
- $^3/_4$ cup (110 g) fresh or frozen blueberries
- $^1/_4$ cup (60 g) unsweetened applesauce

Preheat the oven to 375°F (190°C, or gas mark 5). Spray a muffin tin with nonstick spray.

In a large mixing bowl, combine the sugar or baking sugar substitute, oat bran flour, all-purpose flour, baking powder, baking soda, salt, and lavender. Stir to combine.

In a medium mixing bowl, whisk together the egg, oil, vanilla, yogurt, blueberries, and applesauce, just enough to combine. (The batter should be slightly lumpy.)

Fill the muffin cups two-thirds full with batter. Bake for 20 to 25 minutes, until a toothpick inserted into the middle of a muffin comes out clean. Let the muffins cool for 15 minutes before turning the tin over to release the muffins. (If the muffins stick to the pan, a slight tap on the back should help to release them.)

YIELD: Makes 12 (2-ounce) muffins.

NUTRITIONAL ANALYSIS

Each with: **Calories:** 113.45 **Protein:** 2.94 g **Carbs:** 21.64 g **Total Fat:** 2 g **Sat Fat:** 0.22 g **Cholesterol:** 20.42 mg **Sodium:** 205.71 mg **Sugars:** 9.20 g **Fiber:** 1.39 g

MARGARET'S NOTE

The nutritional analysis is based on the recipe made with table sugar. If you use a sugar substitute instead, the nutritional analysis will be: Calories: 90 Protein: 3 g Carbs: 15 g Total Fat: 2 g Sugars: 2.87 g. (The sugar substitute won't change the fat, cholesterol, sodium, or fiber content.)

Carrot Muffins with Fresh Dill

Serve these savory muffins with soup or salad for a special luncheon.

GBP: Weeks 6–8 Postop

BAND: Weeks 6–8 Postop

BPD: Weeks 6–8 Postop

INGREDIENTS

- ¼ cup (40 g) light brown sugar or brown sugar substitute (see note)
- 1 cup (110 g) oat bran flour
- ½ cup (55 g) all-purpose flour
- 1 teaspoon baking powder
- 1 teaspoon baking soda
- 1 teaspoon onion powder
- ½ teaspoon salt
- 1 egg
- 1 tablespoon (14 ml) vegetable oil
- ⅓ cup (65 g) sugar
- 1 teaspoon lemon juice
- 1 cup (240 g) nonfat plain or vanilla yogurt
- ¾ cup (85 g) finely grated carrots
- 2 tablespoons (4 g) chopped fresh dill
- ¼ cup (60 g) unsweetened applesauce

Preheat the oven to 375°F (190°C, or gas mark 5). Spray a muffin tin with nonstick spray.

In a large mixing bowl, combine the light brown sugar, oat bran flour, all-purpose flour, baking powder, baking soda, onion powder, and salt. Stir to combine.

In a medium mixing bowl, whisk together the egg, oil, sugar, juice, yogurt, carrots, dill, and applesauce, just enough to combine. (The batter should be slightly lumpy.)

Fill the muffin cups two-thirds full with batter. Bake for 20 to 25 minutes, until a toothpick inserted into the middle of a muffin comes out clean. Let the muffins cool for 15 minutes before turning the tin over to release the muffins. (If the muffins stick to the pan, a slight tap on the back should help to release them.)

YIELD: Makes 12 (about 2-ounce) muffins.

NUTRITIONAL ANALYSIS

Each with: **Calories:** 104.71 **Protein:** 3.03 g **Carbs:** 19.5 g **Total Fat:** 2 g **Sat Fat:** 0.22 g **Cholesterol:** 20.42 mg **Sodium:** 215.52 mg **Sugars:** 6.63 g **Fiber:** 1.59 g

MARGARET'S NOTE

If you leave out the brown sugar, each serving will provide: Calories: 90 Protein: 3 g Carbs: 15 g Total Fat: 2 g Sugars: 3 g. (The sugar substitute won't affect the saturated fat, cholesterol, sodium, or fiber.)

Fresh Strawberry Muffins

When strawberries are in season, these muffins are as good for dessert as they are for breakfast.

GBP: Weeks 6-8 Postop

BAND: Weeks 6-8 Postop

BPD: Weeks 6-8 Postop

INGREDIENTS

- ¹/₃ cup (65 g) sugar or ¹/₃ cup (9 g) baking sugar substitute (see page 38) (see note)
- 1 cup (110 g) oat bran flour
- ¹/₂ cup (55 g) all-purpose flour
- 1 teaspoon baking powder
- 1 teaspoon baking soda
- ¹/₂ teaspoon salt
- 1 egg
- 1 tablespoon (14 ml) vegetable oil
- 1¹/₂ teaspoons vanilla extract
- 1 cup (240 g) nonfat vanilla yogurt
- ¹/₄ cup (60 g) unsweetened applesauce
- ³/₄ cup (120 g) sliced fresh strawberries

Preheat the oven to 375°F (190°C, or gas mark 5). Spray a muffin tin with nonstick spray.

In a large mixing bowl, combine the sugar or sugar substitute, oat bran flour, all-purpose flour, baking powder, baking soda, and salt. Stir to combine.

In a medium mixing bowl, whisk together the egg, oil, vanilla, yogurt, and applesauce, just enough to combine. (The batter should be slightly lumpy.) Gently fold in the strawberries.

Fill the muffin cups two-thirds full with batter. Bake for 20 to 25 minutes, until a toothpick inserted into the middle of a muffin comes out clean. Let the muffins cool for 15 minutes before turning the tin over to release the muffins. (If the muffins stick to the pan, a slight tap on the back should help to release them.)

YIELD: Makes 12 (about 2-ounce) muffins.

NUTRITIONAL ANALYSIS

Each with: **Calories:** 111.53 **Protein:** 2.94 g **Carbs:** 21.11 g **Total Fat:** 2 g **Sat Fat:** 0.22 g **Cholesterol:** 20.42 mg **Sodium:** 205.71 mg **Sugars:** 8.79 g **Fiber:** 1.37 g

LYNETTE'S NOTES

For dessert: Slice a muffin in half horizontally and fill the middle with 2 tablespoons (35 g) nonfat, sugar-free vanilla pudding. Replace the top and add a dollop of nonfat whipped cream topping and a few fresh strawberry slices.

MARGARET'S NOTE

If you omit the sugar, each serving will provide: Calories: 88 Protein: 3 g Carbs: 15 g Total Fat: 2 g Sugars: 2 g. (The saturated fat, cholesterol, sodium, and fiber won't change.)

Green Chili and Cheese Cornbread Muffins

These muffins are perfect with soup or chili.

GBP: Weeks 6–8 Postop

BAND: Weeks 6–8 Postop

BPD: Weeks 6–8 Postop

INGREDIENTS

- ¹/₂ cup (55 g) all-purpose flour
- ¹/₂ cup (70 g) coarse yellow cornmeal
- 1 teaspoon baking powder
- ¹/₂ teaspoon baking soda
- ¹/₄ teaspoon salt
- 1¹/₂ teaspoon onion powder
- ¹/₂ cup (120 ml) low-fat buttermilk
- 1 egg
- 2 tablespoons (12 g) diced mild green chilies, drained
- ¹/₂ cup (55 g) reduced-fat shredded Cheddar cheese

Preheat the oven to 400°F (200°C, or gas mark 6). Spray a muffin tin with cooking spray.

In a large mixing bowl, combine the flour, cornmeal, baking powder, baking soda, salt, and onion powder. Stir to combine.

In a medium mixing bowl, whisk together the buttermilk, egg, chiles, and cheese, just enough to combine. (The batter should be slightly lumpy.)

Fill 8 of the muffin cups two-thirds full with batter. Bake for 20 to 25 minutes, until a toothpick inserted into the middle of a muffin comes out clean. Let the muffins cool for 15 minutes before turning the tin over to release the muffins. (If the muffins stick to the pan, a slight tap on the back should help to release them.)

YIELD: Makes 8 (2-ounce) muffins.

NUTRITIONAL ANALYSIS

Each with: **Calories:** 93.10 **Protein:** 4.35 g **Carbs:** 13.36 g **Total Fat:** 2.43 g **Sat Fat:** 1.17 g **Cholesterol:** 34.36 mg **Sodium:** 254.99 mg **Sugars:** 1.09 g **Fiber:** 0.92 g

Zucchini-Bran Muffins

These muffins are great for breakfast or a mid-day snack. They hold well in the freezer for several weeks.

GBP: Weeks 6–8 Postop

BAND: Weeks 6–8 Postop

BPD: Weeks 6–8 Postop

INGREDIENTS

- ⅓ cup (50 g) unpacked light brown sugar or brown sugar substitute (see note)
- ¾ cup (30 g) bran cereal
- 1 cup (110 g) oat bran flour
- ½ cup (55 g) whole wheat flour
- 2 teaspoons baking powder
- ½ teaspoon salt
- 1 teaspoon cinnamon
- ¼ teaspoon nutmeg
- 1 egg
- 1 tablespoon (14 ml) vegetable oil
- ¼ teaspoon vanilla extract
- ¼ teaspoon almond extract
- 1 cup (240 g) nonfat plain or vanilla yogurt
- ¾ cup (95 g) grated zucchini (press out the moisture by squeezing it in paper towels)
- ¼ cup (60 g) unsweetened applesauce

Preheat the oven to 375°F (190°C, or gas mark 5). Spray a muffin tin with cooking spray.

In a large mixing bowl, place the brown sugar or sugar substitute, bran cereal, oat bran flour, whole wheat flour, baking powder, salt, cinnamon, and nutmeg. Stir to combine.

In a medium mixing bowl, whisk together the egg, oil, vanilla, almond extract, yogurt, zucchini, and applesauce, just enough to combine. (The batter should be slightly lumpy.)

Fill the muffin cups two-thirds full with batter. Bake for 20 to 25 minutes, until a toothpick inserted into the middle of a muffin comes out clean. Let the muffins cool for 15 minutes before turning the tin over to release the muffins. (If the muffins stick to the pan, a slight tap on the back should help to release them.)

YIELD: Makes 12 (about 2-ounce) muffins.

NUTRITIONAL ANALYSIS

Each with: **Calories:** 121 **Protein:** 3.8 g **Carbs:** 23.6 g **Total Fat:** 2.18 g **Sat Fat:** 0.26 g **Cholesterol:** 20.42 mg **Sodium:** 157.62 mg **Sugars:** 8.72 g **Fiber:** 3.39 g

MARGARET'S NOTE

If you leave out the brown sugar, each serving of this recipe will provide: Calories: 101 Protein: 4 g Carbs: 18 g Total Fat: 2 g Sugars: 3 g.

Bacon-Cheddar Muffins

You can't go wrong with the flavors of bacon and cheese. To save time, prepare the bacon strips per the package instructions, then chop or break them into crumbles.

GBP: Weeks 6–8 Postop

BAND: Weeks 6–8 Postop

BPD: Weeks 6–8 Postop

INGREDIENTS

- $1/2$ cup (55 g) all-purpose flour
- $1/2$ cup (70 g) coarse yellow cornmeal
- 1 teaspoon baking powder
- $1/2$ teaspoon baking soda
- $1/8$ teaspoon salt
- $1/2$ cup (120 ml) low-fat buttermilk
- 1 egg
- 2 tablespoons (15 g) chopped green onion
- $1/2$ cup (55 g) reduced-fat shredded Cheddar cheese
- $1/4$ cup (20 g) turkey bacon crumbles, prepared as per package instructions (about 4 strips)

Preheat the oven to 375°F (190°C, or gas mark 5). Spray a muffin tin with cooking spray.

In a large mixing bowl, combine the flour, cornmeal, baking powder, baking soda, and salt. Stir to combine.

In a medium mixing bowl, whisk together the buttermilk, egg, green onion, cheese, and bacon, just enough to combine. (The batter should be slightly lumpy.)

Fill 8 of the muffin cups two-thirds full with batter. Bake for 20 to 25 minutes, until a toothpick inserted into the middle of a muffin comes out clean. Let the muffins cool for 15 minutes before turning the tin over to release the muffins. (If the muffins stick to the pan, a slight tap on the back should help to release them.)

YIELD: Makes 8 (2-ounce) muffins.

NUTRITIONAL ANALYSIS

Each with: **Calories:** 101.19 **Protein:** 5.47 g **Carbs:** 12.34 g **Total Fat:** 3.65 g **Sat Fat:** 1.38 g **Cholesterol:** 39.36 mg **Sodium:** 380.42 mg **Sugars:** 0.91 g **Fiber:** 1.01 g

CHAPTER 3

Lunches

Cumin Mushroom Quesadillas

Quesadillas are a great appetizer, or double the amount of mushrooms for a quick and easy entrée. Serve them with Fresh Salsa Caliente (page 132).

GBP: Weeks 6-8 Postop

BAND: Weeks 6-8 Postop

BPD: Weeks 6-8 Postop

INGREDIENTS

- $1/2$ pound (225 g) white or crimini mushrooms
- 1 tablespoon (14 g) low-fat butter alternative
- 1 tablespoon (14 ml) olive oil
- 1 small clove garlic, minced
- 2 teaspoons ground cumin
- $1/8$ teaspoon cayenne pepper (optional)
- $1/4$ teaspoon paprika
- $1/2$ teaspoon kosher salt or sea salt
- 2 tablespoons (25 g) nonfat sour cream
- 4 low-carb whole-wheat tortillas
- $3/4$ cup (85 g) reduced-fat shredded Cheddar cheese
- $1/4$ cup (4 g) chopped fresh cilantro

Clean the mushrooms with a mushroom brush or paper towels. Cut the end of the stems away and discard. Slice the mushrooms into thin pieces.

In a medium nonstick skillet, heat the butter alternative and oil over medium heat. Add the mushrooms, garlic, cumin, pepper (if using), paprika, and salt. Sauté, stirring often, for 8 minutes, until the mushrooms become soft. Stir in the sour cream and continue cooking for 2 minutes, stirring once or twice. Remove the pan from the heat.

Preheat the oven to 375°F (190°C, or gas mark 5). Place the tortillas on a baking sheet. Equally divide the mushrooms on half of each tortilla. Equally divide the cheese and distribute over the mushrooms.

Fold the empty half of each tortilla over the mushroom half. Bake the quesadillas for about 12 minutes, until the cheese has melted.

YIELD: Makes 4 quesadillas.

NUTRITIONAL ANALYSIS

Each with: **Calories:** 168.22 **Protein:** 12.06 g **Carbs:** 16.69 g **Total Fat:** 9.03 g **Sat Fat:** 2.98 g **Cholesterol:** 12.50 mg **Sodium:** 635.33 mg **Sugars:** 1.59 g **Fiber:** 10.19 g

Classic Turkey and Swiss Wrap

Many people have a hard time with breads after any kind of weight-loss surgery, but many of my patients tell me they can tolerate pita bread, wrap or lavash bread, and thin and/or toasted breads. As always when trying a new food for the first time after your weight loss surgery, try only a small amount at a time and listen to your body.

Here's a wrapped version of the classic turkey and Swiss cheese sandwich, only with less carbs, calories, and fat.

GBP: Weeks 6–8 Postop

BAND: Weeks 6–8 Postop

BPD: Weeks 6–8 Postop

INGREDIENTS

- 2 tablespoons (30 g) nonfat mayonnaise
- 2 teaspoons prepared sweet mustard
- $1/8$ teaspoon black pepper
- 4 (9-inch, or 22.5-cm) low-carb tortillas
- 4 whole green or red leaf lettuce leaves
- 12 ounces (340 g) thin sliced roasted turkey, skin and fat removed
- 4 slices (4 ounces, or 115 g) low-fat, low-sodium Swiss cheese
- 2 Italian plum tomatoes, cored and cut lengthwise into 8 slices
- 8 thin red onion ring slices

In a small bowl, combine the mayonnaise, mustard, and pepper. Spread the mixture equally onto 4 tortillas. Next, layer the lettuce, then the turkey, Swiss cheese, tomato, and onion.

Wrap the tortillas tightly around the filing, wrap the roll in plastic wrap, and refrigerate for at least one hour before serving. To serve, cut each wrap in half.

YIELD: Makes 8 ($1/2$-wrap) servings

NUTRITIONAL ANALYSIS

Each with: **Calories:** 151.44 **Protein:** 17.23 g **Carbs:** 11.63 g **Total Fat:** 6.54 g **Sat Fat:** 2.01 g **Cholesterol:** 32.50 mg **Sodium:** 438.73 mg **Sugars:** 2.02 g **Fiber:** 7.31 g

Spinach-Turkey Wraps

These wraps are an easy and nutritious lunch and a great way to use up leftover turkey!

GBP: Weeks 6–8 Postop

BAND: Weeks 6–8 Postop

BPD: Weeks 6–8 Postop

INGREDIENTS

- 4 ounces (115 g) nonfat cream cheese
- 2 tablespoons (15 g) sliced green onions
- 1 teaspoon Dijon mustard
- 4 (9-inch, or 22.5-cm) low-carb tortillas
- 1⅓ cups (40 g) fresh spinach, shredded
- 6 ounces (170 g) thinly sliced roasted turkey breast, skin and fat removed
- ¼ cup (25 g) reduced-fat shredded Cheddar or Jack cheese
- 2 tablespoons (20 g) minced red bell pepper

In a small bowl, combine the cream cheese, green onions, and Dijon mustard.

Spread the mixture equally onto the tortillas. Next, add in equal portions the spinach, turkey, cheese, and bell pepper. Wrap the tortillas tightly around the filing, wrap the rolls in plastic wrap, and refrigerate for at least one hour before serving.

YIELD: Makes 4 wraps.

NUTRITIONAL ANALYSIS

Each with: **Calories:** 184.53 **Protein:** 23.07 g **Carbs:** 21.83 g **Total Fat:** 6.35 g **Sat Fat:** 1.11 g **Cholesterol:** 28.54 mg **Sodium:** 758.59 mg **Sugars:** 1.39 g **Fiber:** 14.47 g

LYNETTE'S NOTES

Wraps are also great for snacks or appetizers. Simply cut each one into fourths for smaller portions.

Classic Turkey, Cranberry, and Cream Cheese Sandwich

This is a refreshing, light sandwich you'll want to give thanks for.

GBP: Weeks 6–8 Postop

BAND: Weeks 6–8 Postop

BPD: Weeks 6–8 Postop

INGREDIENTS

- 2 slices diet whole grain bread, toasted
- 1 teaspoon nonfat mayonnaise
- 2 teaspoons reduced-fat cream cheese
- 2 tablespoons (25 g) cranberry sauce
- 2 ounces (55 g) sliced turkey meat, no skin or fat
- 1 leaf green or red leaf lettuce

On one slice of the bread, spread the mayonnaise, and spread the cream cheese on the other. On top of the cream cheese, spread the cranberry sauce. Place the turkey on top of the cranberry sauce and the lettuce on top of the turkey. Top with the remaining slice of toast and cut in half.

YIELD: Makes 1 (sandwich) serving.

NUTRITIONAL ANALYSIS

Each with: **Calories:** 214.83 **Protein:** 17.28 g **Carbs:** 27.64 g **Total Fat:** 5.08 g **Sat Fat:** 1.49 g **Cholesterol:** 36.67 mg **Sodium:** 640.71 mg **Sugars:** 8.43 g **Fiber:** 5.76 g

Ultimate Veggie Sandwich

A true-blue vegetarian sandwich should contain a few standard ingredients such as avocado, cucumber, and alfalfa sprouts. After that, it's really up to your personal taste. Here's the recipe for my favorite veggie sandwich.

GBP: Weeks 6–8 Postop

BAND: Weeks 6–8 Postop

BPD: Weeks 6–8 Postop

INGREDIENTS

- 2 slices diet whole grain bread, toasted
- $1/4$ ripe avocado (should be slightly soft to the touch on the outside)
- 1 teaspoon nonfat cream cheese
- Small pinch salt
- Small pinch pepper
- 3 thinly sliced red onion rings
- 3 thinly sliced green bell pepper rings
- 2 $5/8$-inch (6.25-cm) thick slices tomato
- 6 thinly sliced cucumber coins, peeled
- 1-inch (2.5-cm) layer alfalfa sprouts

On one slice of bread, spread the avocado, and spread the cream cheese on the other. On top of the avocado, layer the salt, pepper, onion, bell pepper, tomato, cucumber, and sprouts. Top with the remaining slice of bread, spear with toothpicks, cut in half, and serve.

YIELD: Makes 1 (sandwich) serving.

NUTRITIONAL ANALYSIS

Each with: **Calories:** 209.10 **Protein:** 8.05 g **Carbs:** 30.22 g **Total Fat:** 9.02 g **Sat Fat:** 1.76 g **Cholesterol:** 0.76 mg **Sodium:** 291.33 mg **Sugars:** 5.57 g **Fiber:** 10.83 g

Fresh Mozzarella Tomato and Tapenade Sandwich

Tapenade is a delicious (usually pureed) olive spread that can be found in most grocery stores. It's very salty nature is a wonderful complement to the rich creaminess of fresh mozzarella when used in moderation.

GBP: Weeks 6–8 Postop

BAND: Weeks 6–8 Postop

BPD: Weeks 6–8 Postop

- 2 slices diet whole grain bread, toasted
- 2 teaspoons nonfat mayonnaise
- 1 teaspoon olive tapenade
- 2 slices (2 ounces, or 55 g) fresh mozzarella cheese (Press the moisture out a bit with paper towels.)
- 2 ⅝-inch (6.25-cm) thick slices tomato
- Fresh cracked black pepper (optional)

On both slices of bread, spread the mayonnaise evenly. On one slice, spread the tapenade, and then layer the mozzarella, then the tomato. Sprinkle a few turns of pepper on top of the tomatoes (if using). Top with the remaining slice of bread. Spear each corner of the bread with a toothpick about 1 inch (2.5 cm) from the edge of the corner, cut into fourths diagonally, and serve.

YIELD: Makes 1 (sandwich) serving.

NUTRITIONAL ANALYSIS
Each with: **Calories:** 263.70 **Protein:** 14.43 g **Carbs:** 24.70 g **Total Fat:** 13.15 g **Sat Fat:** 0.17 g **Cholesterol:** 40.00 mg **Sodium:** 370.11 mg **Sugars:** 4.87 g **Fiber:** 5.83 g

Baked Ham and Cheese Sandwich

GBP: Weeks 6–8 Postop

BAND: Weeks 6–8 Postop

BPD: Weeks 6–8 Postop

INGREDIENTS

- 2 slices fresh diet whole-grain bread
- 2 teaspoons nonfat mayonnaise
- ½ teaspoon Dijon mustard
- 2 ounces (55 g) reduced-sodium, reduced-fat sliced ham
- 2 ⅝-inch (6.25-cm) thick slices tomato
- 1 slice (1 ounce, or 28 g) reduced-fat Swiss cheese

Preheat the oven to 350°F (180°C, or gas mark 4).

On one slice of bread, spread the mayonnaise and spread the mustard on the other. Place the ham on one slice, then the tomato slices, then the cheese. Top with the remaining slice of bread and place on a sheet pan. Bake the sandwich for about 12 minutes, until the bread is nicely toasted and the cheese is melted. Cut in half and serve warm.

YIELD: Makes 1 (sandwich) serving.

NUTRITIONAL ANALYSIS
Each with: **Calories:** 266.32 **Protein:** 24.23 g **Carbs:** 26.99 g **Total Fat:** 8.21 g **Sat Fat:** 2.98 g **Cholesterol:** 43.00 mg **Sodium:** 812.66 mg **Sugars:** 3.83 g **Fiber:** 6.14 g

MARGARET'S NOTE

This recipe is high in sodium because of the ham. If sodium is a problem for you, substitute 2 ounces (55 g) of low-sodium turkey or roast beef for the ham in this sandwich.

Leftover Salmon Sandwich

Delicious and satisfying flavor doesn't get any easier than this! However you prepared your salmon dinner, this easy recipe will make it just as delicious for lunch.

GBP: Weeks 6–8 Postop

BAND: Weeks 6–8 Postop

BPD: Weeks 6–8 Postop

INGREDIENTS

- 6 ounces (170 g) leftover salmon, skin and bones removed
- 1 tablespoon (15 g) nonfat mayonnaise
- 2 whole-grain English muffin halves, toasted
- 2 ⅝-inch (6.25-cm) thick tomato slices

In a small bowl, mix the salmon with the mayonnaise. Top each muffin half with a tomato slice, then the salmon mixture, and serve.

YIELD: Makes 2 (½-sandwich) servings.

NUTRITIONAL ANALYSIS
Each with: **Calories:** 228.31 **Protein:** 24.59 g **Carbs:** 14.82 g **Total Fat:** 7.66 g **Sat Fat:** 1.18 g **Cholesterol:** 60.35 mg **Sodium:** 306.33 mg **Sugars:** 3.79 g **Fiber:** 2.38 g

Turkey Sandwich with Cucumbers and Herbed Cream Cheese

This sandwich is light and refreshing.

GBP: Weeks 6–8 Postop

BAND: Weeks 6–8 Postop

BPD: Weeks 6–8 Postop

INGREDIENTS

- 2 ounces (55 g) nonfat cream cheese
- ¼ teaspoon chopped fresh chives
- ¼ teaspoon chopped fresh tarragon
- ¼ teaspoon chopped fresh parsley
- 2 slices diet whole-grain bread, toasted
- 6 thinly sliced cucumber coins, peeled
- 2 ounces (55 g) sliced turkey breast, no skin or fat

In a small bowl, mix together the cream cheese, chives, tarragon, and parsley. Spread half of the mixture on each slice of the bread.

Place the cucumber evenly atop the cream cheese mixture, then place the turkey on top of the cucumber. Top with the remaining slice of bread and serve.

YIELD: Makes 1 (sandwich) serving.

NUTRITIONAL ANALYSIS
Each with: **Calories:** 221.74 **Protein:** 24.68 g **Carbs:** 24.46 g **Total Fat:** 3.92 g **Sat Fat:** 0.68 g **Cholesterol:** 34.54 mg **Sodium:** 865.28 mg **Sugars:** 2.29 g **Fiber:** 5.87 g

Awesome Egg Salad Sandwich

Here's an "egg-citing" sandwich indeed!

GBP: Weeks 6–8 Postop

BAND: Weeks 6–8 Postop

BPD: Weeks 6–8 Postop

INGREDIENTS

- 2 whole hard-boiled eggs
- 2 hard-boiled eggs, whites only
- 2 teaspoons nonfat mayonnaise
- $1/4$ teaspoon Dijon mustard
- 1 teaspoon finely chopped chives
- $1/8$ teaspoon celery seed
- 2 whole-grain English muffin halves, toasted

In a small bowl, crush the hard-boiled eggs and egg whites with a fork. Add the mayonnaise, mustard, chives, and celery seed and mix to combine. Top each muffin half with half of the egg salad and serve.

YIELD: Makes 2 ($1/2$ sandwich) servings.

NUTRITIONAL ANALYSIS
Each with: **Calories:** 164.78 **Protein:** 13.40 g **Carbs:** 14.57 g **Total Fat:** 5.79 g **Sat Fat:** 1.61 g **Cholesterol:** 240.01 mg **Sodium:** 364.78 mg **Sugars:** 4.07 g **Fiber:** 2.11 g

Bacon, Tomato, Lettuce, and Cream Cheese Sandwich

Add cream cheese to this standard for a delightful combination of flavors.

GBP: Weeks 6–8 Postop

BAND: Weeks 6–8 Postop

BPD: Weeks 6–8 Postop

INGREDIENTS

- 2 slices diet whole grain bread, toasted
- 1 ounce (28 g) nonfat cream cheese
- 2 strips reduced-sodium, reduced-fat turkey bacon or veggie bacon
- 2 $5/8$-inch (6.25-cm) thick slices tomato
- 2 red or green leaf lettuce leaves, stems removed
- Fresh cracked black pepper (optional)

On each slice of bread, evenly spread the cream cheese. Place the bacon strips in a cross from corner to corner on one slice. Layer the tomato, the pepper (if using), then the lettuce leaves, and top with the remaining slice of bread. Spear each half of the sandwich with a toothpick, cut in half, and serve.

YIELD: Makes 1 (sandwich) serving.

NUTRITIONAL ANALYSIS
Each with: **Calories:** 186.63 **Protein:** 12.66 g **Carbs:** 23.50 g **Total Fat:** 6.55 g **Sat Fat:** 1.43 g **Cholesterol:** 22.27 mg **Sodium:** 773.58 mg **Sugars:** 2.64 g **Fiber:** 5.98 g

Best Ever Tofu Burger

Serve with whole wheat and/or low-carb whole-grain pita bread.

GBP: Weeks 4–6 Postop

BAND: Weeks 4–6 Postop

BPD: Weeks 3–6 Postop

INGREDIENTS

- 2 pounds (910 g) firm tofu (but not silken tofu), frozen at least 48 hours
- ¹/₂ cup (120 ml) water
- 2 tablespoons (28 ml) soy sauce or mushroom soy sauce
- 2 tablespoons (30 g) ketchup
- 2 teaspoons Marmite, Vegemite, or other yeast extract (gives a "beefy" flavor) or 4 teaspoons red miso
- ¹/₄ teaspoon fresh minced garlic (one small clove)
- ¹/₄ teaspoon dried oregano
- ¹/₄ teaspoon dried basil
- 2 tablespoons (20 g) minced fresh onion
- 6 ¹/₈-inch- (3 mm-) thick slices tomato
- 6 leaves red leaf lettuce
- 12 slices whole-wheat bread or 6 low-carb, whole grain pitas

Thaw out the tofu. Slice each pound block into 3 thick slices. Place the slices on a cookie sheet covered with a couple of clean, folded tea towels. Cover the slices with more tea towels and another cookie sheet. Weigh this arrangement down with something heavy for about 30 minutes. Place the tofu in a single layer in a shallow container.

In a medium bowl, combine the water, soy sauce, ketchup, yeast extract, garlic, oregano, basil, and onion and pour over the prepared tofu slices. Cover and let marinate for at least 2 hours. (The tofu can marinate for up to 24 hours.)

Spray a heavy skillet or nonstick skillet with cooking spray. Heat it over medium-high heat. Pan-fry the tofu until browned on both sides. Top with the tomato and lettuce. Serve with the bread or pitas.

YIELD: Makes 6 (about 3-ounce) burgers.

NUTRITIONAL ANALYSIS

Each with: **Calories:** 150.68 **Protein:** 16.14 g **Carbs:** 6.98 g **Total Fat:** 6.54 g **Sat Fat:** 0.98 g **Cholesterol:** 0.00 mg **Sodium:** 221.77 mg **Sugars:** 3.43 g **Fiber:** 1.35 g

Zesty Turkey Burger Pita Pocket

GBP: Weeks 6-8 Postop

BAND: Weeks 6-8 Postop

BPD: Weeks 6-8 Postop

INGREDIENTS

- ½ cup (80 g) diced onion
- ⅓ cup (80 g) low-sodium, low-carb ketchup
- 1 teaspoon lemon-pepper seasoning
- 1 teaspoon cumin seed
- ¼ teaspoon cinnamon
- ⅛ teaspoon black pepper
- 1 tablespoon chopped fresh cilantro
- 1 pound (455 g) extra lean ground turkey (97% fat-free, contains no skin)
- 4 (4-inch, or 10-cm) whole wheat pita pockets
- 4 teaspoons nonfat mayonnaise
- 4 ⅛-inch (3-mm) thick tomato slices
- 4 red leaf lettuce leaves

Preheat the oven to 300°F (150°C, or gas mark 2).

In a medium mixing bowl, combine the onion, ketchup, lemon-pepper seasoning, cumin, cinnamon, pepper, cilantro, and turkey and mix thoroughly. Divide the turkey mixture into 4 equal portions, shaping each into a 1-inch- (2.5-cm-) thick patty.

Place a medium nonstick skillet over medium-heat until hot. Add the patties and cook for about 6 minutes on each side, until no longer pink. Remove burgers from the pan and let rest for 5 minutes.

Wrap the pita pockets in aluminum foil and bake for 10 minutes. Spread 1 teaspoon of mayonnaise inside each pita pocket. Place one burger patty in each pita pocket and top each patty with a slice of tomato and lettuce. Serve immediately.

YIELD: Makes 4 sandwiches.

NUTRITIONAL ANALYSIS

Each with: **Calories:** 239.88 **Protein:** 30.77 g **Carbs:** 25.71 g **Total Fat:** 2.70 g **Sat Fat:** 0.65 g **Cholesterol:** 55.00 mg **Sodium:** 273.07 mg **Sugars:** 6.91 g **Fiber:** 3.15 g

Asian Chicken Wrap

This is a delicious treat worthy of your favorite Asian restaurant. Eaten from the hands, theses wraps are a hit with kids.

GBP: Weeks 6–8 Postop

BAND: Weeks 6–8 Postop

BPD: Weeks 6–8 Postop

INGREDIENTS

- 1 tablespoon (14 ml) peanut oil
- 1 tablespoon (14 ml) toasted sesame oil
- 1 tablespoon (14 ml) rice vinegar
- 1 tablespoon (14 ml) low-sodium soy sauce
- 1 teaspoon garlic-chili sauce
- 1 teaspoon fresh grated ginger
- 1/2 teaspoon orange zest (grated orange peel)
- 1 clove fresh garlic, minced
- 4 (4 ounce, or 115 g) boneless, skinless chicken breast halves
- 1 cup (25 g) fresh mint leaves, coarsely chopped
- 1 cup (30 g) fresh baby spinach leaves, stems removed
- 1/2 cup (8 g) cilantro sprigs
- 1/2 cup (50 g) mung bean sprouts
- 8 whole Boston lettuce leaves (about 1 head)
- 1 lime, cut into 8 wedges
- 1 tablespoon (10 g) chopped peanuts (optional)

In a small bowl, combine the peanut oil, sesame oil, vinegar, soy sauce, garlic-chili sauce, ginger, orange zest, and garlic and stir vigorously with a wire whisk. Reserve 2 tablespoons (28 ml) of the mixture and place the rest in a zipper-type plastic bag along with the chicken and marinate in the refrigerator for 1 hour, turning once or twice. Remove the chicken from the bag and discard the marinade.

Coat a medium skillet with nonstick spray and heat it over medium-high heat. Add the chicken to the pan and cook for 6 minutes on each side. Remove the chicken from the pan and let stand while preparing the filling.

In a medium mixing bowl, combine the mint, spinach, cilantro, and bean sprouts. Add the reserved oil mixture and gently toss, just enough to expose all the surface area to the dressing, being careful not to break down the leafy structure.

Slice the chicken into thin strips. Place one sliced chicken breast atop one (or two stacked) lettuce leaves, then top the chicken with the spinach mixture. Garnish equally with chopped peanuts (if using).

YIELD: Makes 4 servings (about 3 ounces chicken and 1/4 cup vegetables each).

NUTRITIONAL ANALYSIS

Each with: **Calories:** 196.76 g **Protein:** 29.01 g **Carbs:** 5.79 g **Total Fat:** 6.30 g **Sat Fat:** 0.84 g **Cholesterol:** 65.77 mg **Sodium:** 194.29 mg **Sugars:** 2.19 g **Fiber:** 2.65 g

Pita Pizza

Pizza is always a crowd pleaser. Follow these instructions or vary the ingredients to satisfy your pickiest palate.

GBP: Weeks 6-8 Postop

BAND: Weeks 6-8 Postop

BPD: Weeks 6-8 Postop

INGREDIENTS

- 4 small (4-inch, or 10 cm) pita breads (whole wheat, preferably)
- 1 can (6 ounces, or 170 g) low-sodium tomato paste
- 1 teaspoon dried oregano
- 1 teaspoon dried basil
- 1 teaspoon dried thyme
- 4 tablespoons (20 g) grated Parmesan cheese
- 1 cup (140 g) cooked, boneless, skinless chicken breast, cut into $1/2$-inch (1.25-cm) cubes
- $1/2$ cup (30 g) sliced fresh mushrooms
- 1 can ($2^{1}/2$ ounces, or 70 g) sliced olives, drained
- $3/4$ cup (85 g) shredded part-skim mozzarella cheese

Preheat the oven to 375°F (190°C, or gas mark 5). Lightly spray a sheet pan with cooking spray.

Place the pita breads on the sheet pan. Spread about 2 tablespoons (30 g) tomato paste evenly onto each pita bread. Distribute the oregano, basil, thyme, Parmesan, chicken, mushrooms, olives, and mozzarella evenly onto the pizzas. Bake the pizzas for about 15 minutes, until the cheese is bubbly and begins to brown.

YIELD: Makes 4 (4-inch) pizzas.

NUTRITIONAL ANALYSIS

Each with: **Calories:** 284.45 **Protein:** 25.61 g **Carbs:** 24.80 g **Total Fat:** 9.39 g **Sat Fat:** 4.07 g **Cholesterol:** 47.14 mg **Sodium:** 538.32 mg **Sugars:** 5.50 g **Fiber:** 5.09 g

Variations

- In place of the chicken, try a pepperoni alternative (such as soy or vegetable), chicken Italian sausage (skins removed and pre-cooked), leanest ground turkey or beef (precooked and drained of excess grease and liquid).

- In place of the mushrooms and olives, try steamed asparagus tips, drained and sliced artichoke hearts, fresh Roma tomato slices, or fresh spinach leaves.

Fall Harvest Pumpkin Soup

This soup is delicious, fun, and a great source of vitamin A. Include the curry powder and cayenne pepper if you like a lot of heat.

GBP: Weeks 2-4 Postop

BAND: Weeks 2-4 Postop

BPD: Weeks 2-4 Postop

INGREDIENTS

- 3 cups (735 g) pureed canned pumpkin (no salt) or 1 (5-pound, or 2.5 kg) sugar pumpkin
- 1 large yellow onion, diced
- 2 large celery ribs cut into ¹/₂-inch (1.25-cm) pieces
- 1 quart (1 L) low-sodium chicken stock
- ¹/₂ cup (120 ml) white wine, cooking sherry, chicken broth, or vegetable broth
- 2 teaspoons cinnamon, plus more for garnish (optional)
- 2 teaspoons allspice
- 2 teaspoons curry powder (optional)
- 2 teaspoons paprika
- ¹/₂ teaspoon cumin
- 1 teaspoon cayenne pepper (optional)
- ¹/₂ teaspoon ground white pepper
- ³/₄ cup (175 ml) nonfat half-and-half (see note)

If using fresh pumpkin, preheat the oven to 375°F (190°C, or gas mark 5).

Cut the pumpkin in half and scrape out the seed and strings. Cut the halves into quarters. Place the pumpkin, skin-side down, in a 9¹/₂- x 13¹/₂-inch (22.5- x 32.5-cm) or 3-quart (3-L) baking dish, with about ¹/₂ inch (1.25 cm) of water in it. Bake the pumpkin for about 60 minutes, until the flesh is tender throughout. Let it cool and scrape out the flesh.

Puree the pumpkin using a hand mixer, blender, or food processor. (You'll have about 3 cups puree.)

In a 4-quart (4-L) soup pot, place the chicken stock, onion, and celery. Cover and bring it to a simmer. Continue cooking for about 15 minutes, until the vegetables are soft and translucent. With a slotted spoon or small mesh strainer, remove the vegetables and puree using the same method as the pumpkin. Return the vegetables to the chicken stock and add the pumpkin puree. Add the wine (or sherry or broth), cinnamon, allspice, curry powder (if using), paprika, cumin, cayenne pepper (if using), and white pepper. Slowly stir in the half-and-half. Bring it back to a simmer and continue cooking for about 20 minutes, stirring occasionally. Serve in warmed soup bowls, and garnish with a light sprinkle of cinnamon (if using).

YIELD: Makes 6 (1-cup) servings.

NUTRITIONAL ANALYSIS

Each with: **Calories:** 151.17 **Protein:** 5.82 g **Carbs:** 21.99 g **Total Fat:** 3.58 g **Sat Fat:** 0.72 g **Cholesterol:** 4.54 mg **Sodium:** 252.18 mg **Sugars:** 7.44 g **Fiber:** 5.13 g

MARGARET'S NOTE

If you use light half-and-half instead of nonfat, the sugar content will increase to 9 grams per serving, which is still within the 14 grams or less per serving as my general recommendation for weight-loss surgery patients. However, if you use low-sugar, the sugar content will decrease to 3 grams per serving. The taste difference may or may not be noticeable, depending on your individual preferences. Either one is nutritionally acceptable.

Chilled Honeydew Soup with Spearmint

This cold soup is a summertime crowd-pleaser! It can be served as an appetizer, between courses to cleanse the palate, or as a light dessert.

GBP: Weeks 2-4 Postop

BAND: Weeks 2-4 Postop

BPD: Weeks 2-4 Postop

INGREDIENTS

- 1 honeydew melon
- ¹⁄₄ cup (60 ml) lemon juice
- ¹⁄₂ cup (120 ml) cooking sherry or alcohol-free white wine
- 2 tablespoons (11 g) chopped spearmint leaves
- 8 sprigs fresh spearmint (optional)

Cut the melon in half and scrape out and discard the seeds. Using a tablespoon, scrape all of the flesh into a food processor fitted with a metal S blade. Add the lemon juice, sherry or wine, and chopped spearmint. Puree the mixture just until it has a liquid consistency. Place it into a 3-quart (3-L) container with an airtight lid and chill it in the refrigerator for at least 1 hour. Stir and serve in chilled dessert bowls or martini glasses. Garnish with the spearmint sprigs (if using).

YIELD: Makes 8 (about ¹⁄₂-cup) servings.

NUTRITIONAL ANALYSIS:

Each with: **Calories:** 73.60 **Protein:** 0.94 g **Carbs:** 15.39 g **Total Fat:** 0.23 g **Sat Fat:** 0.06 g **Cholesterol:** 0.00 mg **Sodium:** 114.35 mg **Sugars:** 13.25 g **Fiber:** 1.41 g

MARGARET'S NOTE

The serving size above is half the usual serving of soups in this book because the content of sugars is too high using the 1-cup serving (because of the fruit). The ¹⁄₂-cup serving provides 13 grams of sugars, which is within the 14 grams or less per serving needed to avoid dumping syndrome. Gastric banding patients, or those who are not sensitive to sugars, can enjoy a larger portion (such as 1 cup), because this is a low-fat, healthy soup.

Lentil Soup

Rich in fiber, protein, and iron, this soup is tasty, too.

GBP: Weeks 2-4 Postop

BAND: Weeks 2-4 Postop

BPD: Weeks 2-4 Postop

INGREDIENTS

- 1 tablespoon (14 ml) extra-virgin olive oil
- 1 cup (130 g) diced carrot (about 1 large)
- ³/₄ cup (120 g) diced yellow onion (about 1 medium)
- 1 cup (100 g) diced celery (about 1 large rib)
- 2 cloves fresh garlic, chopped
- 2 bay leaves
- 1 tablespoon (14 ml) low-sodium tamari soy sauce
- ¹/₂ teaspoon black pepper
- 1 teaspoon dried oregano
- 1 teaspoon dried thyme
- 1 can (14.5 ounces, or 415 g) plum tomatoes, drained
- 2 cups (385 g) green lentils, soaked for 30 minutes (see note)
- 4¹/₂ cups (1 L) water
- Water or low-sodium vegetable broth (optional)
- 6 sprigs fresh thyme

In a 3-quart (3-L) stockpot or soup pot over medium-high heat, heat the oil. Add the carrot, onion, celery, garlic, bay leaves, tamari soy sauce, pepper, oregano, and dried thyme, and cook until the carrots begin to soften. Break apart the tomatoes by crushing them with your hands, then add them to the pot. Drain the lentils, and then add them to the pot. Add the water and bring to a boil. Reduce the heat to a soft boil, cover partially, and cook for 20 minutes, until the lentils become soft throughout. If a thinner consistency is desired, add additional water or low-sodium vegetable broth in small amounts at a time. (Adding too much water to the soup will decrease the strength in flavor.) Remove the bay leaves prior to serving. Garnish with the thyme sprigs and serve in warmed soup bowls.

YIELD: Makes about 6 (1-cup) servings.

NUTRITIONAL ANALYSIS

Each with: **Calories:** 312.58 **Protein:** 20.20 g **Carbs:** 48.78 g **Total Fat:** 4.91 g **Sat Fat:** 1.04 g **Cholesterol:** 0.00 mg **Sodium:** 393.70 mg **Sugars:** 10.79 g **Fiber:** 23.14 g

MARGARET'S NOTE

Although lentils are high in protein, they need to be soaked for at least 30 minutes to help remove the phytates (natural mineral binders) that might impede the absorption of iron.

Creamy Tomato Parmesan Soup

GBP: Weeks 2–4 Postop

BAND: Weeks 2–4 Postop

BPD: Weeks 2–4 Postop

INGREDIENTS

- 1 cup (150 g) peeled and diced Yukon Gold potatoes (about 1 large potato)
- 1/2 cup (80 g) diced yellow onion (about 1/2 large onion)
- 2 cloves garlic, chopped
- 1/2 teaspoon basil
- 1/2 teaspoon oregano
- 1/4 teaspoon black pepper
- 1/4 teaspoon salt
- 2 cans (14.5 ounces, or 415 g each) diced tomatoes in juice (no salt added)
- 1/2 cups (120 ml) 2% milk
- 1/4 cup (60 ml) plain low-fat yogurt
- 2 tablespoons (10 g) grated Parmesan cheese
- 1 tablespoon (4 g) chopped fresh parsley

In a 2-quart (2-L) saucepan, place the potatoes, onion, garlic, basil, oregano, pepper, and salt with enough water to cover 1 inch (2.5 cm) above the level of the vegetables. Bring to a boil, then reduce the heat and simmer uncovered for about 15 minutes, until the potatoes are tender throughout.

Drain the tomatoes, reserving the juice. Place the tomatoes in a food processor or blender and puree. Add the tomatoes and juice to the saucepan.

In a separate 4-cup (1-L) mixing bowl, mix the milk, yogurt, and cheese, stirring until a smooth consistency is reached.

Bring the soup to a simmer and slowly add the yogurt-milk mixture, stirring vigorously with a wire whip until all ingredients are evenly incorporated. Serve in warmed soup bowls and garnish with the parsley.

YIELD: Makes 4 (1- cup) servings.

NUTRITIONAL ANALYSIS

Each with: **Calories:** 92.39 **Protein:** 6.82 g **Carbs:** 15.21 g **Total Fat:** 1.36 g **Sat Fat:** 0.80 g **Cholesterol:** 4.75 mg **Sodium:** 363.65 mg **Sugars:** 8.24 g **Fiber:** 2.63 g

Black Bean Soup

High in fiber, this is super tasty, too!

GBP: Weeks 2–4 Postop

BAND: Weeks 2–4 Postop

BPD: Weeks 2–4 Postop

INGREDIENTS

- ¹/₂ cup (90 g) long-grain brown rice, raw, rinsed, and drained
- 1 cup (235 ml) water
- 2 cans (16 ounces, or 455 g each) black beans, drained
- 1 tablespoon (14 ml) olive oil
- 1 medium onion, diced
- 1 tablespoon (6 g) finely chopped jalapeño pepper
- 2 cloves garlic, minced
- 1¹/₂ teaspoons ground cumin
- ¹/₂ teaspoon cayenne pepper (optional)
- 1 teaspoon oregano
- 1 teaspoon paprika
- 1 teaspoon chili powder
- 1 can (11 ounces, or 310 g) diced tomatoes, drained
- 1¹/₂ quarts (1.5 L) low-sodium chicken broth
- Juice of ¹/₂ fresh lime
- 2 tablespoons (2 g) chopped fresh cilantro
- 1 cup (115 g) reduced-fat shredded Cheddar cheese

In a 1-quart (1-L) saucepan, place the rice and water and bring to a boil.

Immediately reduce the heat to a simmer, then loosely cover and simmer for about 15 minutes, until all the liquid is absorbed. Remove from the heat.

In a food processor, puree the beans and set aside.

In a 3-quart (3-L) saucepan, heat the oil over medium-high heat. Add the onion, jalapeno, garlic, cumin, cayenne pepper (if using), oregano, paprika, and chili powder and sauté until the onion begins to soften. Add the tomatoes and stir. Add the pureed beans, rice, broth, and lime juice and stir with a wire whip. Bring to a soft simmer and continue cooking for 20 minutes, stirring once every 5 minutes. Serve in warmed soup bowls and garnish with the cilantro and cheese.

YIELD: Makes 8 (about 1-cup) servings.

NUTRITIONAL ANALYSIS

Each with: **Calories:** 206.02 **Protein:** 11.28 g **Carbs:** 29.66 g **Total Fat:** 4.38 g **Sat Fat:** 2.21 g **Cholesterol:** 10.00 mg **Sodium:** 535.08 mg **Sugars:** 2.51 g **Fiber:** 5.76 g

Potato Leek Soup with Fresh Tarragon

GBP: Weeks 2–4 Postop

BAND: Weeks 2–4 Postop

BPD: Weeks 2–4 Postop

INGREDIENTS

- 1½ to 2 cups (225 to 300 g) peeled and diced russet potatoes
- 1³/₄ pounds (795 g) leeks (2 large or 3 medium)
- 2 tablespoons (28 g) margarine or light butter (see note)
- 2 cloves garlic, minced
- 1 teaspoon black pepper
- 5 cups (40 ounces, or 1185 ml) low-sodium chicken broth
- ¼ cup (15 g) fresh, coarsely chopped tarragon leaves
- 4 to 6 whole tarragon sprigs (optional)

In a 2-quart (2-L) saucepan, cover the potatoes with water and bring it to a boil. Continue cooking for about 12 minutes, until the potatoes are tender throughout. Remove from the heat and drain in a colander. Set aside.

Cut the green tops away from the leeks and discard them. Split the white portions of the leeks down the middle, leaving just the roots intact, and wash them clean of all sand and grit. Drain in a colander. Slice the leeks into thin half-coins. Discard the roots and set aside.

In a 4-quart (4-L) soup pot, melt the margarine over medium heat. Add the leeks, garlic, and pepper and cook until the leeks are tender, but not brown. Add the broth, potatoes, and tarragon leaves and bring to a simmer over low heat. Cook for about 15 minutes. Remove from the heat and let cool for about 15 minutes. With a slotted spoon, remove three-quarters of the solid ingredients and place in a blender or food processor. Blend until smooth. Return the mixture to the soup pot. Heat and stir to an even consistency. Serve in warmed soup bowls and garnish with the tarragon sprigs (if using).

YIELD: Makes 5 (about 1-cup) servings.

NUTRITIONAL ANALYSIS

Each with: **Calories:** 186.63 **Protein:** 5.24 g **Carbs:** 36.71 g **Total Fat:** 3.05 g **Sat Fat:** 0.51 g **Cholesterol:** 0.00 mg **Sodium:** 96.93 mg **Sugars:** 6.73 g **Fiber:** 4.57 g

LYNETTE'S NOTE

Try to find a light margarine or butter that has the same consistency and flavor as real butter. It may cost a bit more, but there are some good substitutes available.

Sweet Potato Soup

GBP: Weeks 2–4 Postop

BAND: Weeks 2–4 Postop

BPD: Weeks 2–4 Postop

INGREDIENTS

- 2 quarts (64 ounces, or 2-L) low-sodium chicken or vegetable broth, plus more to thin soup (optional)
- 1 quart (1-L) water
- 4 medium to large sweet potatoes, peeled and cut into approximately 1-inch (2.5-cm) cubes
- 3 cups (480 g) diced large yellow onion (about 2 large)
- 3 medium carrots, peeled and sliced into coins
- 2 large ribs celery, sliced into approximately 1-inch (2.5-cm) pieces
- ¼ cup (60 ml) lemon juice (about 1 lemon)
- 3 teaspoons ground caraway seed
- 3 teaspoons dry mustard
- ½ teaspoon cayenne pepper (optional)
- ¼ cup (15 g) chopped fresh parsley
- ½ teaspoon black pepper
- ½ teaspoon salt
- Nonfat plain yogurt or nonfat sour cream (optional)

Pour the broth and water into a 6-quart (6-L) stockpot or Dutch oven. Add the sweet potato, onion, carrots, and celery. Cover the pot and bring it to a boil. Continue boiling about 25 minutes, until the potatoes are soft. (They should fall apart when speared with a fork.) Remove the pot from the heat and let it stand for about 15 minutes. With a slotted spoon, remove all the solids from the pot and place them in a food processor fitted with a metal S blade or a blender and puree. Reserve the liquid in the pot. (Unless you have an industrial-size processor, this requires more than one batch.) Return the puree to the remaining liquid in the pot. Add the lemon juice, caraway, mustard, cayenne pepper (if using), and parsley. Cover the pot and slowly bring to a simmer. Continue simmering for 20 minutes, stirring often. Check seasonings and adjust with the salt and pepper. If a thinner consistency is desired, add additional chicken or vegetable broth in small amounts until the desired consistency is reached. Serve in warmed bowls and garnish with a dollop yogurt or sour cream (if using).

YIELD: Makes 8 (1½-cup) servings.

NUTRITIONAL ANALYSIS

Each with: **Calories:** 113.68 **Protein:** 3.40 g **Carbs:** 24.55 g **Total Fat:** 0.54 g **Sat Fat:** 0.05 g **Cholesterol:** 0.00 mg **Sodium:** 200.15 mg **Sugars:** 6.87 g **Fiber:** 4.23 g

Vegetarian Vegetable Soup

This is completely vegetarian. When soup is just what you need, you just can't beat a bowl of homemade vegetable soup. This soup can easily be frozen in smaller portions for later enjoyment.

GBP: Weeks 2–4 Postop

BAND: Weeks 2–4 Postop

BPD: Weeks 2–4 Postop

INGREDIENTS

- 3 cloves garlic
- Juice of 1 lemon
- 1$^1/_2$ teaspoon cayenne pepper (optional)
- 1 cup (100 g) diced celery
- 1 large carrot, diced
- 1 cup (125 g) diced zucchini
- 1 large yellow onion, diced
- $^1/_2$ cup (75 g) fresh or frozen peas
- 1$^1/_2$ cups (225 g) peeled, diced fresh tomato (see note)
- 2 quarts (64 ounces, or 2-L) low-sodium vegetable broth (see note)
- 2 medium red potatoes, skinned and diced into $^1/_4$-inch (6-mm) cubes
- $^1/_2$ teaspoon black pepper
- $^1/_4$ teaspoon salt

Place all of the ingredients into a large pot and bring to a rolling (rapid) boil. Reduce heat to a soft boil and continue cooking uncovered about 30 minutes, until the dense vegetables are done. The tomatoes can be added toward the end to hold the form longer.

YIELD: Makes 10 (about 1$^1/_2$-cup) servings.

NUTRITIONAL ANALYSIS
Each with: **Calories:** 70.01 **Protein:** 2.87 g **Carbs:** 14.40 g **Total Fat:** 0.28 g **Sat Fat:** 0.04 g **Cholesterol:** 0.00 mg **Sodium:** 95.85 mg **Sugars:** 3.16 g **Fiber:** 2.45 g

NOTE

To peel the tomatoes, score the bottoms with an X and then blanch them. (Drop them into boiling water just long enough to peel back the skins and remove them from the water.) Let cool to the touch. The skins will come right off.

LYNETTE'S NOTE

If you prefer to make a homemade stock instead of using a store-bought one, and you find the flavor is not to your satisfaction, continue cooking uncovered to reduce the liquid. This will condense your soup and intensify the flavor.

MARGARET'S NOTE

If you're having a hard time getting enough protein into your diet, and this soup is a meal for you, add 2 ounces (55 g) of high-protein powder. (Make sure it's appropriate for hot liquids and add it after heating the soup, just before eating it to preserve the quality of the protein.) This can increase the protein content to more than 20 grams per serving. However, it won't be vegetarian. To keep it strictly vegetarian, or vegan, use a rice or soy protein powder.

CHAPTER 5

Salads

Whole-Wheat Elbow Macaroni Salad

Bring this pasta salad to a potluck or barbecue. Garnish it with fresh tomato wedges.

GBP: Weeks 6–8 Postop

BAND: Weeks 6–8 Postop

BPD: Weeks 6–8 Postop

INGREDIENTS

- 1 cup (105 g) dry whole-wheat macaroni
- ½ cup (115 g) nonfat mayonnaise
- 1 teaspoon Dijon mustard
- 1 tablespoon (14 ml) lemon juice
- 1 teaspoon celery salt
- ½ teaspoon black pepper
- ½ cup (80 g) finely chopped red onion
- ¾ cup (75 g) finely chopped celery
- ½ cup (70 g) finely chopped red bell pepper
- 1 tablespoon (9 g) sliced black olives
- 1 tablespoon (4 g) chopped fresh parsley
- 1½ teaspoons finely chopped green onion

Cook the macaroni according to package instructions, omitting the salt and oil. Drain the macaroni and cool completely in the refrigerator.

While the macaroni cools, place the mayonnaise, mustard, lemon juice, celery salt, and pepper in a small mixing bowl and stir to combine.

When the pasta is completely cooled, place it in a large mixing bowl along with the onion, celery, bell pepper, olives, parsley, and green onion and pour the dressing over the top. Using a large spoon or rubber spatula, gently stir the pasta until it is completely covered with dressing. Transfer to a serving bowl.

YIELD: Makes about 8 (½-cup) servings.

NUTRITIONAL ANALYSIS

Each with: **Calories:** 69.92 **Protein:** 2.41 g **Carbs:** 14.32 g **Total Fat:** 0.51 g **Sat Fat:** 0.05 g **Cholesterol:** 0.01 mg **Sodium:** 156.99 mg **Sugars:** 3.14 g **Fiber:** 1.96 g

Classic Spinach Salad
with Apple Cider Vinaigrette

This can be served as a side salad or an entrée. It's perfect for a light summer dinner. Make the dressing at least 20 minutes ahead of time. It's great topped with toasted slivered almonds.

GBP: Weeks 6–8 Postop

BAND: Weeks 6–8 Postop

BPD: Weeks 6–8 Postop

INGREDIENTS

- 2 tablespoons (28 ml) olive oil
- 1 tablespoon (14 ml) apple cider vinegar
- 1 tablespoon (14 ml) fresh lemon juice
- 1 medium clove fresh garlic, cut into thin slivers
- $1/2$ teaspoon low-sodium soy sauce
- $1/4$ teaspoon black pepper
- 8 $1/8$-inch- (3-mm-) thick red onion rings
- 8 cups (240 g) fresh baby spinach, washed and thoroughly drained and dried
- 4 strips turkey bacon, cooked crisp and crumbled
- 1 small cucumber, peeled and thinly sliced
- 4 Italian plum tomatoes, cored and cut into 4 wedges each
- 2 hard-boiled eggs, cooled, peeled, and cut into 4 wedges each

In a glass jar with a tightly fitting lid, place the oil, vinegar, lemon juice, garlic, soy sauce, and pepper. Shake vigorously. Set aside.

About 20 minutes before serving, place the onion in the jar of salad dressing to marinate.

In a large mixing bowl, place the spinach, bacon, and cucumber.

Remove the onion from the dressing and set aside. Pour the dressing evenly over the salad and gently toss, just enough to ensure complete coverage. Distribute the dressed salad evenly in the center of 4 entrée plates or 8 side salad plates. Place the tomato wedges leaning against the outer edges of each salad. Place the egg wedges next to the tomato wedges. Top the salads with 1 or 2 onion rings. Serve immediately.

YIELD: Makes 8 ($1/2$-cup) servings or 4 (1 cup) servings.

NUTRITIONAL ANALYSIS

Each with: **Calories:** 90.46 **Protein:** 3.86 g **Carbs:** 5.79 g **Total Fat:** 6.10 g **Sat Fat:** 1.14 g **Cholesterol:** 65.00 mg **Sodium:** 163.85 mg **Sugars:** 2.11 g **Fiber:** 1.80 g

Mandarin Pea Pod Salad

This salad is colorful, nutritious, and wonderful for home entertaining.

GBP: Weeks 6–8 Postop

BAND: Weeks 6–8 Postop

BPD: Weeks 6–8 Postop

INGREDIENTS

- 2 packages (10 ounces, 280 g each) prewashed fresh spinach
- 2 cups (475 ml) water
- 2 cups (about ³/₄ pound, 340 g) fresh snow peas
- 2 cups (500 g) canned mandarin oranges, drained
- 2 tablespoons (15 g) toasted sesame seeds (optional)
- 2 tablespoons (20 g) thinly sliced shallots
- 1 tablespoon (14 ml) extra-virgin olive oil
- ¹/₄ cup (60 ml) apple cider vinegar
- ¹/₄ teaspoon salt
- ¹/₄ teaspoon black pepper
- 2 tablespoons (28 ml) fresh lime juice (from about ¹/₂ lime)
- 1 teaspoon lime zest (grated peel of about ¹/₂ lime)

Cut the stems off of the spinach and shred (with your hands) into about 1-inch (2.5-cm) pieces, arranging evenly on a serving platter.

In a 1¹/₂ -quart (1.5-L) saucepan, bring the water to a boil. Remove the stems and strings from the peas.

Prepare an ice bath by filling a medium mixing bowl with ice and just enough cold water to cover. Drop the peas into the boiling water and blanch them for about 45 seconds. With a strainer, remove the peas and immediately place them into the ice bath. (This stops the cooking process and helps to maintain beautiful, bright green color.) After 60 seconds in the ice bath, remove the peas, drain, pat dry with paper towels, and place evenly atop the spinach. Arrange the mandarin oranges evenly over the peas.

In a small plastic container with a lid, combine the sesame seeds (if using), shallots, oil, vinegar, salt, pepper, lime juice, and lime zest. Shake vigorously and/or whisk until the dressing is emulsified. Just prior to serving, pour the salad dressing evenly over the top.

YIELD: Makes 8 (about ³/₄-cup) servings.

NUTRITIONAL ANALYSIS

Each with: **Calories:** 102.22 **Protein:** 3.49 g **Carbs:** 17.09 g **Total Fat:** 2.44 g **Sat Fat:** 0.32 g **Cholesterol:** 0.00 mg **Sodium:** 99.57 mg **Sugars:** 11.76 g **Fiber:** 3.72 g

"This salad went over very well with us and our friends. The flavors were a great and refreshing combination."

—Jill and Dan,
gastric banding surgery patients in the Washington, D.C., area

Hearts of Palm Salad
with Arugula and Endive

Try topping this salad with grilled chicken, shrimp, or pork tenderloin cut into thin strips.

GBP: Weeks 6–8 Postop

BAND: Weeks 6–8 Postop

BPD: Weeks 6–8 Postop

INGREDIENTS

- Zest and juice of $1/2$ lime
- 1 tablespoon (14 ml) apple cider vinegar
- 1 tablespoon (14 ml) fresh orange juice
- $1/8$ teaspoon fresh minced garlic
- Pinch cayenne pepper (optional)
- 2 tablespoons (28 ml) olive oil
- 3 teaspoons chopped fresh cilantro
- 3 cups (60 g) arugula, washed and dried
- 1 medium Belgium endive, cut into bite-size pieces
- 1 small radicchio, cut into bite-size pieces
- 4 stalks canned hearts of palm, cut into 1-inch (2.5-cm) match sticks
- $1/2$ fresh mango, cut into about 1-inch (2.5-cm) strips

In a small mixing bowl, place the lime zest and lime juice. Add the vinegar, orange juice, garlic, and cayenne pepper (if using). Whisk with a wire whip to combine. Continue whisking while slowly adding the oil until the dressing is emulsified. Add the cilantro and stir. Set aside for the flavors to marry while preparing the salad.

In a salad bowl, place the arugula. Add the endive and radicchio. Top with the hearts of palm and mango. Toss with the dressing just before serving.

YIELD: Makes 6 (about $3/4$-cup) servings.

NUTRITIONAL ANALYSIS
Each with: **Calories:** 87.56 **Protein:** 2.43 g **Carbs:** 9.42 g **Total Fat:** 5.16 g **Sat Fat:** 0.78 g **Cholesterol:** 0.00 mg **Sodium:** 122.06 mg **Sugars:** 3.67 g **Fiber:** 3.93 g

Marinated Mushroom and Tomato Salad with Dijon Vinaigrette

This salad is a great side dish for beef entrees.

GBP: Weeks 6–8 Postop

BAND: Weeks 6–8 Postop

BPD: Weeks 6–8 Postop

INGREDIENTS

- 1 pound (455 g) 1-inch (2.5-cm) button or crimini mushrooms
- 8 large ripe Roma tomatoes
- ¼ cup (40 g) thinly sliced red onion
- ¼ cup (60 ml) olive oil
- 1 tablespoon (14 ml) balsamic vinegar
- 1 teaspoon sugar
- 1 tablespoon (15 g) Dijon mustard
- 2 tablespoons (6 g) finely chopped fresh chives
- ½ teaspoon sea salt or kosher salt
- ¼ teaspoon fresh cracked black pepper
- 2 whole chive stems

Clean the mushrooms with a mushroom brush or paper towels. Cut the end of the stems away and discard. Cut the mushrooms into halves.

Core the tomatoes and cut them in half length-wise, then slice into ¼-inch (6 mm) half-circles.

In a medium mixing bowl, place the mushrooms, tomatoes, and onion and set aside.

In a small mixing bowl, combine the oil, vinegar, sugar, mustard, chopped chives, salt, and pepper and stir vigorously with a wire whisk. Allow the dressing to sit for at least 10 minutes to marry the flavors.

Pour the dressing over the salad and gently toss to ensure complete coverage. Transfer the salad to a serving bowl and garnish with the chive stems in the shape of an X against the rim of the bowl.

YIELD: Makes 12 (about ½-cup) servings.

NUTRITIONAL ANALYSIS

Each with: **Calories:** 73.75 **Protein:** 2.01 g **Carbs:** 5.92 g **Total Fat:** 5.17 g **Sat Fat:** 0.73 g **Cholesterol:** 0.03 mg **Sodium:** 64.00 mg **Sugars:** 3.66 g **Fiber:** 1.44 g

Mexican Shrimp Salad with Jicama

This south-of-the-border salad combines shrimp with jicama, a refreshing flavor with a unique and crunchy texture.

GBP: Weeks 6–8 Postop

BAND: Weeks 6–8 Postop

BPD: Weeks 6–8 Postop

INGREDIENTS

- $1/3$ cup (35 g) thinly sliced green onions
- $1/3$ cup (75 g) nonfat mayonnaise
- $1/3$ cup (80 g) nonfat plain yogurt
- 2 teaspoon red pepper sauce
- 1 tablespoon chopped fresh cilantro
- 2 teaspoons prepared horseradish
- 1 teaspoon chili powder
- 1 teaspoon ground cumin
- 2 teaspoons lime juice
- $1^{1}/_{2}$ pounds (680 g) pre-cooked medium-size shrimp
- $1/2$ medium jicama, skinned and cut into about 1/2-inch (2.5-cm) pieces (about $3/4$ cup, or 90 g)
- 4 cups (80 g) hearty salad greens, ready to serve
- 2 tablespoons (28 ml) low-calorie Thousand Island dressing (prepared or on this page)

In a medium mixing bowl, place the green onions, mayonnaise, yogurt, pepper sauce, cilantro, horseradish, chili powder, cumin, and lime juice and stir to combine. Add the shrimp and toss to cover with the dressing. Cover the bowl and refrigerate to marinate for 30 to 60 minutes. Add the jicama and stir to coat. Discard excess marinade.

In another medium mixing bowl, toss the salad greens with the Thousand Island dressing and shrimp. Serve on chilled salad plates.

YIELD: Makes about 6 (1-cup) servings.

NUTRITIONAL ANALYSIS
Each with: **Calories:** 155.42 **Protein:** 24.34 g **Carbs:** 8.22 g **Total Fat:** 2.12 g **Sat Fat:** 0.38 g **Cholesterol:** 172.65 mg **Sodium:** 365.22 mg **Sugars:** 3.48 g **Fiber:** 2.18 g

Thousand Island Dressing

GBP: Weeks 2–4 Postop

BAND: Weeks 2–4 Postop

BPD: Weeks 2–4 Postop

INGREDIENTS

- 1 cup (225 g) nonfat cottage cheese
- $1/3$ cup (75 ml) low-fat buttermilk
- 1 teaspoon fresh lemon juice
- 2 tablespoons (30 g) sweet pickle relish
- 1 teaspoon red pepper sauce
- 1 tablespoon (15 g) low-carb ketchup

Place all of the ingredients in a blender or food processor and blend until smooth.

YIELD: Makes 10 (about 2-tablespoon) servings.

NUTRITIONAL ANALYSIS
Each with: **Calories:** 24.20 **Protein:** 2.89 g **Carbs:** 2.81 g **Total Fat:** 0.09 g **Sat Fat:** 0.05 g **Cholesterol:** 1.33 mg **Sodium:** 131.54 mg **Sugars:** 1.62 g **Fiber:** 0.04 g

Greek Salad

This is the perfect accompaniment to Kosher Lamb Souvlaki (page 204).

GBP: Weeks 6–8 Postop

BAND: Weeks 6–8 Postop

BPD: Weeks 6–8 Postop

INGREDIENTS

- 2 medium to large cucumbers
- 1 large green bell pepper
- 1 medium red onion, cut into ¼-inch (6-mm) strips
- 2 tomatoes, cored and diced into 1-inch (2.5-cm) cubes
- ½ cup (70 g) whole Greek olives
- ¾ cup (115 g) feta cheese, cut into ½-inch (1.25-mm) cubes, or feta cheese crumbles
- 2 tablespoons (28 ml) olive oil
- 2 teaspoons lemon juice
- 2 teaspoons red wine vinegar
- 2 teaspoons chopped fresh thyme leaves, stems removed
- ⅛ teaspoon salt
- ⅛ teaspoon cracked black pepper
- Bundle fresh thyme

Using a vegetable peeler, remove the cucumber skins and cut the cucumbers in half, length-wise. Remove the seeds using a spoon to scrape down the middle. Slice the peeled, seeded cucumbers into ¼- to ½-inch (6- to 12-mm) pieces and place them in a large mixing bowl.

Core the bell pepper, remove the membrane, and cut it into ½-inch (1.25-cm) pieces and add them to the cucumbers. Add the onion, tomato, olives, and cheese and set aside.

In a medium mixing bowl, combine the oil, lemon juice, vinegar, thyme, salt, and black pepper. Stir vigorously with a wire whip until the dressing is emulsified. Pour the dressing over the salad and mix thoroughly. Place the salad in a serving bowl and garnish it with a bundle of fresh thyme.

YIELD: Makes 8 (about 1-cup) servings.

NUTRITIONAL ANALYSIS

Each with: **Calories:** 116.97 **Protein:** 3.15 g **Carbs:** 6.96 g **Total Fat:** 8.36 g **Sat Fat:** 2.64 g **Cholesterol:** 12.52 mg **Sodium:** 286.38 mg **Sugars:** 4.02 g **Fiber:** 1.60 g

Leftover Salmon Salad

This is a great way to use up leftover salmon. Served on just a small portion of greens, it is ideal for lunch.

GBP: Weeks 4–6 Postop

BAND: Weeks 4–6 Postop

BPD: Weeks 3–6 Postop

INGREDIENTS

- 6 ounces (170 g) cold leftover salmon
- 6 small black olives, sliced
- 1 tablespoon (16 g) finely chopped celery
- 1 tablespoon (10 g) finely chopped red bell pepper
- 1$\frac{1}{2}$ teaspoons finely chopped red onion
- 1 teaspoon chopped fresh parsley
- 2 cups (40 g) salad greens, washed, drained, and dried with paper towels
- 1$\frac{1}{2}$ tablespoons (20 ml) low-fat, low-carb salad dressing (prepared or see pages 126 to 129)
- 1 Italian plum tomato, cored and cut into 4 wedges

Flake the salmon apart with a fork, removing any skin or bones, and place it in a small mixing bowl. Add the olives, celery, pepper, onion, and parsley and mix gently, just enough to combine.

In a small mixing bowl, place the salad greens. Pour the salad dressing over the greens and gently toss to expose all of the surface area to the dressing. Equally distribute the greens onto 2 plates and top with the salmon mixture. Garnish each salad with 2 tomato wedges and serve.

YIELD: Makes 2 (3-ounce salmon, $\frac{1}{2}$-cup salad) servings.

NUTRITIONAL ANALYSIS

Each with: **Calories:** 162.99 **Protein:** 17.99 g **Carbs:** 6.21 g **Total Fat:** 7.06 g **Sat Fat:** 0.85 g **Cholesterol:** 46.78 mg **Sodium:** 276.78 mg **Sugars:** 3.53 g **Fiber:** 2.03 g

Radicchio and Cauliflower Salad with Roasted Walnuts

This colorful, festive salad is great for home entertaining or everyday enjoyment.

GBP: Weeks 6–8 Postop

BAND: Weeks 6–8 Postop

BPD: Weeks 6–8 Postop

INGREDIENTS

- 1 tablespoon (8 g) finely chopped walnuts
- 1 large radicchio head, quartered lengthwise, then sliced crosswise into thin strips
- 1 small cauliflower head, cut into small florets
- 1/2 small red onion, thinly sliced (about 1/3 cup, or 35 g)
- 1/2 cup (4 ounces, or 115 g) feta cheese
- 1 clove garlic, minced
- 1 tablespoon (14 ml) balsamic vinegar
- 1 teaspoon Dijon mustard
- 2 teaspoons minced shallot
- 1 teaspoon chopped fresh oregano
- 2 tablespoons (28 ml) olive oil
- 1/8 teaspoon salt
- 1 pinch freshly ground black pepper

Preheat the oven to 375°F (190°C, or gas mark 5).

Place the walnuts on a sheet pan and bake for about 12 minutes, until the walnuts just begin to brown. Remove the sheet pan from the oven and set aside, allowing nuts to cool completely before adding them to the salad.

In a large bowl, mix the radicchio, cauliflower, and onion. Crumble the feta over the salad.

In a small bowl, whisk together the garlic, vinegar, mustard, shallot, and oregano. Slowly whisk in the oil. Season with the salt and pepper and mix the dressing into the salad. Let the salad sit for 1 hour in the refrigerator and top with toasted walnuts just prior to serving.

YIELD: Makes 6 (about 1/2-cup) servings.

NUTRITIONAL ANALYSIS
Each with: **Calories:** 109.52 **Protein:** 4.70 g **Carbs:** 5.65 g **Total Fat:** 8.35 g **Sat Fat:** 3.29 g **Cholesterol:** 16.68 mg **Sodium:** 293.74 mg **Sugars:** 3.09 g **Fiber:** 1.55 g

Roasted Beets and Mango Salad

GBP: Weeks 6–8 Postop

BAND: Weeks 6–8 Postop

BPD: Weeks 6–8 Postop

INGREDIENTS

- 2 medium beets, peeled and cut into 1-inch (2.5-cm) cubes (about ³/₄ pound, or 340 g)
- ¹/₄ (60 ml) cup 100% orange juice
- 2 tablespoons (28 ml) fresh lime juice
- ¹/₂ teaspoon black pepper
- 1 tablespoon (15 g) Dijon mustard
- 2 teaspoons extra-virgin olive oil
- ¹/₈ teaspoon sea salt or kosher salt
- 1 cup (165 g) cubed ripe mango (about 2 mangoes)
- 6 cups (120 g) mixed field greens or gourmet salad mix

Preheat the oven to 425°F (220°C, or gas mark 7).

In a 2-quart (2-L) saucepan, place the beets and cover with water to 1 inch (2.5 cm) above the level of the beets. Boil for 7 minutes, and then drain the beets in a colander.

Spray a 7¹/₂- x 11¹/₂-inch (17.5- x 27.5-cm) baking dish with cooking spray. Place the beats in the dish and roast for 30 minutes, until the beets are tender. Place beets in mixing bowl and cool in refrigerator.

In a 1 quart (1-L) mixing bowl, combine the orange juice, lime juice, pepper, mustard, oil, and salt. Mix vigorously with a wire whip or a fork and divide into two equal portions. Add one portion of the dressing to the beets and toss to cover all of the beet surface.

Remove the beets, reserving the remaining dressing. Combine the two portions of the remaining dressing.

In a large mixing bowl, place the salad greens. Pour the dressing over the salad greens. Gently toss to ensure complete exposure of the greens to the dressing.

Add the mangos to the beets and gently fold just enough to disperse beets and mangos evenly.

Divide the salad mixture among six chilled salad plates and top each salad with an equal amount of the beet-mango mixture.

YIELD: Makes 6 (about 1-cup) servings.

NUTRITIONAL ANALYSIS

Each with: **Calories:** 63.92 **Protein:** 1.52 g **Carbs:** 11.88 g **Total Fat:** 1.90 g **Sat Fat:** 0.25 g **Cholesterol:** 0.00 mg **Sodium:** 98.43 mg **Sugars:** 8.67 g **Fiber:** 2.65 g

Watercress Salad with Tarragon and Mint Leaves

This is perfect as an accompaniment to Baked Sea Bass (page 186).

GBP: Weeks 6-8 Postop

BAND: Weeks 6-8 Postop

BPD: Weeks 6-8 Postop

INGREDIENTS

- 1 tablespoon (14 ml) olive oil
- 3 tablespoons (45 ml) apple cider vinegar
- 2 teaspoons lemon juice
- $1/4$ teaspoon salt
- $1/4$ teaspoon black pepper
- 2 cups (70 g) watercress
- $1/4$ cup (6 g) fresh spearmint leaves
- $1/4$ cup (15 g) fresh tarragon leaves

In a small bowl, combine the oil, vinegar, and lemon juice and whisk briefly until emulsified. Add the salt and pepper.

In a serving bowl, place the watercress, mint, and tarragon. Pour the dressing on top and gently toss with salad tongs, just enough to ensure complete coverage.

YIELD: Makes 4 servings.

NUTRITIONAL ANALYSIS

Each with: **Calories:** 42.44 **Protein:** 1.03 g **Carbs:** 4.96 g **Total Fat:** 3.69 g **Sat Fat:** 0.55 g **Cholesterol:** 0.00 mg **Sodium:** 98.07 mg **Sugars:** 3.10 g **Fiber:** 0.64 g

Creamy Lemon Herb Dressing

This low-fat (non-oil-based) salad dressing is the perfect alternative to the same old store-bought flavors. Making delicious salad dressing is really just this simple!

GBP: Weeks 2–4 Postop

BAND: Weeks 2–4 Postop

BPD: Weeks 2–4 Postop

INGREDIENTS

- 1 cup (225 g) nonfat cottage cheese
- 1/3 cup (75 ml) low-fat buttermilk
- 2 teaspoons fresh lemon juice
- 1/2 teaspoon lemon zest
- 1 teaspoon chopped fresh tarragon leaves
- 1 teaspoon chopped fresh parsley
- 1 teaspoon chopped fresh green onion (white and green parts)

Place all of the ingredients in a blender or food processor and blend until smooth.

YIELD: Makes 10 (about 2-tablespoon) servings.

NUTRITIONAL ANALYSIS

Each with: **Calories:** 19.84 **Protein:** 2.90 g **Carbs:** 1.74 g **Total Fat:** 0.08 g **Sat Fat:** 0.05 g **Cholesterol:** 1.33 mg **Sodium:** 96.71 mg **Sugars:** 1.42 g **Fiber:** 0.03 g

Blue Cheese Dressing

GBP: Weeks 2–4 Postop

BAND: Weeks 2–4 Postop

BPD: Weeks 2–4 Postop

INGREDIENTS

- 1 cup (225 g) nonfat cottage cheese
- 1/3 cup (75 ml) nonfat buttermilk
- 2 tablespoons (15 g) blue cheese crumbles
- 1/2 teaspoon Worcestershire sauce
- 1/2 teaspoon fresh lemon juice
- 1 teaspoon finely chopped fresh parsley
- 1/2 teaspoon black pepper

Place all of the ingredients in a blender or food processor and blend until smooth.

YIELD: Makes 10 (about 2-tablespoon) servings.

NUTRITIONAL ANALYSIS

Each with: **Calories:** 24.88 **Protein:** 3.23 g **Carbs:** 1.76 g **Total Fat:** 0.51 g **Sat Fat:** 0.29 g **Cholesterol:** 2.33 mg **Sodium:** 115.72 mg **Sugars:** 1.43 g **Fiber:** 0.03 g

Creamy Italian Dressing

GBP: Weeks 2–4 Postop

BAND: Weeks 2–4 Postop

BPD: Weeks 2–4 Postop

INGREDIENTS

- 1 cup (225 g) nonfat cottage cheese
- $^1/_3$ cup (75 ml) low-fat buttermilk
- 1 teaspoon fresh lemon juice
- $^1/_2$ teaspoon dried basil
- $^1/_2$ teaspoon dried oregano
- $^1/_2$ teaspoon dried thyme
- $^1/_2$ teaspoon garlic powder

Place all of the ingredients in a blender or food processor and blend until smooth.

YIELD: Makes 10 (about 2-tablespoon) servings.

NUTRITIONAL ANALYSIS

Each with: **Calories:** 20.34 **Protein:** 2.93 g **Carbs:** 1.82 g **Total Fat:** 0.08 g **Sat Fat:** 0.05 g **Cholesterol:** 1.33 mg **Sodium:** 96.69 mg **Sugars:** 1.44 g **Fiber:** 0.05 g

French Dressing

GBP: Weeks 2–4 Postop

BAND: Weeks 2–4 Postop

BPD: Weeks 2–4 Postop

INGREDIENTS

- 1 cup (225 g) nonfat cottage cheese
- $^1/_3$ cup (75 ml) low-fat buttermilk
- $1^1/_2$ teaspoons paprika
- $^1/_2$ teaspoon Worcestershire sauce
- 2 teaspoons unsalted tomato juice
- 1 teaspoon onion powder
- $^1/_2$ teaspoon dry mustard

Place all of the ingredients in a blender or food processor and blend until smooth.

YIELD: Makes 10 (about 2-tablespoon) servings.

NUTRITIONAL ANALYSIS

Each with: **Calories:** 21.80 **Protein:** 3.01 g **Carbs:** 2.05 g **Total Fat:** 0.18 g **Sat Fat:** 0.05 g **Cholesterol:** 1.33 mg **Sodium:** 97.03 mg **Sugars:** 1.58 g **Fiber:** 0.14 g

Sweet Lemon Poppy Seed Dressing

GBP: Weeks 2–4 Postop

BAND: Weeks 2–4 Postop

BPD: Weeks 2–4 Postop

INGREDIENTS

- 1 cup (225 g) nonfat cottage cheese
- 1/3 cup (75 ml) low-fat buttermilk
- 2 teaspoons fresh lemon juice
- 1/2 teaspoon lemon zest
- 2 teaspoons honey
- 1 teaspoon poppy seeds

Place all of the ingredients in a blender or food processor and blend until smooth.

YIELD: Makes 10 (about 2-tablespoon) servings.

NUTRITIONAL ANALYSIS

Each with: **Calories:** 25.06 **Protein:** 2.93 g **Carbs:** 2.83 g **Total Fat:** 0.20 g **Sat Fat:** 0.06 g **Cholesterol:** 1.33 mg **Sodium:** 96.65 mg **Sugars:** 2.52 g **Fiber:** 0.04 g

Garden Goddess Dressing

GBP: Weeks 2–4 Postop

BAND: Weeks 2–4 Postop

BPD: Weeks 2–4 Postop

INGREDIENTS

- 1 cup (225 g) nonfat cottage cheese
- 1/3 cup (75 ml) low-fat buttermilk
- 1 teaspoon fresh lemon juice
- 2 teaspoons anchovy paste
- 1 tablespoon (4 g) chopped fresh parsley
- 2 teaspoons chopped green onion
- 1 teaspoon chopped fresh oregano leaves (stems removed)

Place all of the ingredients in a blender or food processor and blend until smooth.

YIELD: Makes 10 (about 2-tablespoon) servings.

NUTRITIONAL ANALYSIS

Each with: **Calories:** 21.94 **Protein:** 3.04 g **Carbs:** 1.75 g **Total Fat:** 0.25 g **Sat Fat:** 0.08 g **Cholesterol:** 4.99 mg **Sodium:** 159.49 mg **Sugars:** 1.42 g **Fiber:** 0.07 g

Dill Dressing

GBP: Weeks 2–4 Postop

BAND: Weeks 2–4 Postop

BPD: Weeks 2–4 Postop

INGREDIENTS

- 1 cup (225 g) nonfat cottage cheese
- $1/3$ cup (75 ml) low-fat buttermilk
- 1 teaspoon fresh lemon juice
- $1^1/2$ tablespoons (3 g) chopped fresh dill
- $1/4$ teaspoon black pepper
- $1/4$ teaspoon ground celery seed

Place all of the ingredients in a blender or food processor and blend until smooth.

YIELD: Makes 10 (about 2-tablespoon) servings.

NUTRITIONAL ANALYSIS

Each with: **Calories:** 19.87 **Protein:** 2.90 g **Carbs:** 1.70 g **Total Fat:** 0.09 g **Sat Fat:** 0.05 g **Cholesterol:** 1.33 mg **Sodium:** 96.73 mg **Sugars:** 1.40 g **Fiber:** 0.02 g

Horseradish Dressing

This one really packs a punch!

GBP: Weeks 2–4 Postop

BAND: Weeks 2–4 Postop

BPD: Weeks 2–4 Postop

INGREDIENTS

- 1 cup (225 g) nonfat cottage cheese
- $1/3$ cup (75 ml) low-fat buttermilk
- 1 teaspoon fresh lemon juice
- 1 tablespoon (15 g) fresh grated horseradish
- 1 teaspoon chopped fresh parsley
- 1 teaspoon chopped fresh green onion (white parts only)

Place all of the ingredients in a blender or food processor and blend until smooth.

YIELD: Makes 10 (about 2-tablespoon) servings.

NUTRITIONAL ANALYSIS

Each with: **Calories:** 19.72 **Protein:** 2.89 g **Carbs:** 1.71 g **Total Fat:** 0.07 g **Sat Fat:** 0.05 g **Cholesterol:** 1.33 mg **Sodium:** 96.92 mg **Sugars:** 1.41 g **Fiber:** 0.03 g

CHAPTER 6

Appetizers and Entertaining at Home

Vegetable Party Platter

Serve with the delicious Smoked Salmon Dip (page 140) for a festive dish.

GBP: Weeks 6–8 Postop

BAND: Weeks 6–8 Postop

BPD: Weeks 6–8 Postop

INGREDIENTS

- 8 whole leaves red leaf lettuce
- 1 red bell pepper, cut into strips
- 1 yellow bell pepper, cut into strips
- 3 Italian plum tomatoes, cored and cut into 4 wedges each
- $1/2$ cauliflower head, cut into bite-size florets

On a large serving platter, spread out the lettuce leaves. Arrange the vegetable pieces around the outside of the bowl.

YIELD: Makes 12 (about $1/4$-cup) servings.

NUTRITIONAL ANALYSIS

Each with: **Calories:** 25.66 **Protein:** 1.30 g **Carbs:** 5.46 g **Total Fat:** 0.23 g **Sat Fat:** 0.04 g **Cholesterol:** 0.00 mg **Sodium:** 12.80 mg **Sugars:** 3.43 g **Fiber:** 1.95 g

Sweet Corn Relish

Try this zesty relish as a topping for fish or chicken or for a dip with Toasted Pita Chips (page 136).

GBP: Weeks 4–6 Postop

BAND: Weeks 4–6 Postop

BPD: Weeks 3–6 Postop

INGREDIENTS

- $1^1/2$ cups (240 g) fresh corn kernels (about 4 large ears, shucked)
- $1/2$ medium red bell pepper, cored and finely chopped (about $1/2$ cup, or 70 g)
- 2 tablespoons (20 g) finely chopped red onion
- 1 teaspoon finely chopped fresh jalapeno pepper, seeds removed
- 2 teaspoons chopped fresh cilantro
- 1 small clove garlic, minced
- 1 teaspoon salt
- $1/4$ teaspoon black pepper

In a small bowl, combine all ingredients and stir to mix. Cover and refrigerate for 30 minutes, stirring once or twice before serving.

YIELD: Makes 8 (about $1/4$-cup) servings.

NUTRITIONAL ANALYSIS

Each with: **Calories:** 38.95 **Protein:** 1.25 g **Carbs:** 8.86 g **Total Fat:** 0.43 g **Sat Fat:** 0.06 g **Cholesterol:** 0.00 mg **Sodium:** 42.17 mg **Sugars:** 1.87 g **Fiber:** 1.24 g

Curry Yogurt Dip

Serve with Toasted Pita Chips (page 136) and fresh vegetable sticks. It can be made up to 24 hours ahead of time.

GBP: Weeks 2–4 Postop

BAND: Weeks 2–4 Postop

BPD: Weeks 2–4 Postop

INGREDIENTS

- 1 cup (225 g) nonfat cottage cheese
- 3 tablespoons (45 g) nonfat mayonnaise
- 1 green onion, thinly sliced (white and green parts)
- 3 teaspoons chopped fresh cilantro
- 1½ teaspoons curry powder
- ⅛ teaspoon cayenne pepper (optional)

In a food processor, blend the cottage cheese for about 30 seconds, until smooth.

Using a rubber spatula, scrape the cottage cheese into a small mixing bowl and add the mayonnaise, onion, cilantro, curry powder, and cayenne pepper (if using). Stir to combine, place in a serving bowl, cover, and refrigerate until ready to serve.

YIELD: Makes 8 (about 2-tablespoons) servings.

NUTRITIONAL ANALYSIS

Each with: **Calories:** 25.43 **Protein:** 3.33 g **Carbs:** 2.57 g **Total Fat:** 0.06 g **Sat Fat:** 0.01 g **Cholesterol:** 1.25 mg **Sodium:** 155.32 mg **Sugars:** 1.67 g **Fiber:** 0.19 g

Fresh Salsa Caliente

GBP: Weeks 4–6 Postop

BAND: Weeks 4–6 Postop

BPD: Weeks 3–6 Postop

INGREDIENTS

- 1 cup (180 g) coarsely chopped tomato
- $\frac{1}{4}$ cup (40 g) coarsely chopped yellow or red onion
- 1 small jalapeno pepper, finely chopped (optional)
- 2 tablespoons (2 g) chopped fresh cilantro
- $\frac{1}{4}$ teaspoon salt
- $\frac{1}{4}$ teaspoon cracked black pepper

Place the tomato, onion, and jalapeno pepper (if using) in a food processor fitted with a metal blade. Pulse the mixture just enough to break the pieces down to a bit smaller size. Add the cilantro, salt, and pepper and pulse one or two more times.

YIELD: Makes 6 (about $\frac{1}{4}$-cup) servings.

NUTRITIONAL ANALYSIS
Each with: **Calories:** 11.98 **Protein:** 0.47 g **Carbs:** 2.62 g **Total Fat:** 0.16 g **Sat Fat:** 0.02 g **Cholesterol:** 0.00 mg **Sodium:** 71.84 mg **Sugars:** 1.39 g **Fiber:** 0.64 g

Hot Artichoke Dip

This is a simple, healthy, delicious dip that will get your party started right. I make it for parties, and it's always a hit! For added color and a little more flavor, add 1 tablespoon (10 g) finely chopped red pepper. For a little extra kick, add 1 finely chopped small fresh jalapeno pepper. For more fiber, serve with low-fat, whole wheat crackers.

GBP: Weeks 4–6 Postop

BAND: Weeks 4–6 Postop

BPD: Weeks 4–6 Postop

INGREDIENTS

- 2 cans (14 ounces, 400 g each) artichoke hearts, drained and cut into quarters
- 1 cup (110 g) shredded low-moisture, part-skim mozzarella cheese
- $^3/_4$ cup (175 g) nonfat mayonnaise
- $^1/_4$ cup (20 g) shredded Parmesan cheese
- $^1/_8$ teaspoon salt
- $^1/_4$ teaspoon black pepper

Preheat the oven to 375°F (190°C, or gas mark 5).

In a 1-quart (1-L) casserole oven-safe dish, place the artichoke hearts. Add the mozzarella cheese, mayonnaise, Parmesan cheese, salt, and pepper. Mix thoroughly with a large spoon, ensuring even distribution. Bake the dip for 15 minutes and serve immediately. (Avoid overheating to ensure the mayonnaise does not separate.)

YIELD: Makes 10 (about $^1/_2$-cup) servings.

NUTRITIONAL ANALYSIS
Each with: **Calories:** 74.47 **Protein:** 4.97 g **Carbs:** 7.30 g **Total Fat:** 2.35 g **Sat Fat:** 1.55 g **Cholesterol:** 7.44 mg **Sodium:** 456.30 mg **Sugars:** 1.87 g **Fiber:** 1.21 g

Toasted Pita Chips

Pita chips are a great alternative to high-fat corn or potato chips and can be flavored in a variety of ways. This recipe is plain and simple to complement the scrumptious flavor of Roasted Garlic below.

GBP: Weeks 6–8 Postop

BAND: Weeks 6–8 Postop

BPD: Weeks 6–8 Postop

INGREDIENTS

- 1 tablespoon (14 ml) olive oil
- 6 (6-inch, or 15 cm) whole-wheat pita breads
- ½ teaspoon celery salt
- ½ teaspoon paprika
- ⅛ teaspoon black pepper

Preheat the oven to 375°F (190°C, or gas mark 5). Using a pastry brush, lightly brush oil onto both sides of each pita. Cut the pitas into 8 wedges each. In a small bowl, combine the celery salt, paprika, and pepper. Place the pitas on a baking sheet and sprinkle one side with the seasoning mixture. Bake the pitas for about 15 minutes, until the chips are beginning to turn golden brown.

YIELD: Makes 48 chips; 1 serving is about 4 pita chips.

MARGARET'S NOTE

You could use low-carb whole-wheat pita bread instead of regular whole-wheat pita to lower the calories and increase the protein of the pita chips.

Roasted Garlic

Roasted garlic is versatile and easy to prepare. (It's also easy on the breath after it's cooked!) In addition to the Toasted Pita Chips (above), try spreading some on a toasted English muffin with scrambled egg substitute for breakfast.

INGREDIENTS

- 10 garlic bulbs
- Olive oil

Preheat the oven to 300°F (150°C, or gas mark 2). Peel away the papery skin on the outside of the garlic bulbs, but leave the cloves attached. Rub some olive oil on your hands, then rub the whole bulbs of garlic just enough to give them a slightly shiny appearance. Wrap the bulbs in aluminum foil and place on a sheet pan. Roast the garlic for 1 hour, until the cloves are soft. (You will surely smell it cooking before it's done!) Unwrap the garlic and allow it to cool to the touch before squeezing out the soft, delicious pulp.

YIELD: 12 servings

NUTRITIONAL ANALYSIS

Each with: **Calories:** 100.00 **Protein:** 3.31 g **Carbs:** 18.49 g **Total Fat:** 2.02 g **Sat Fat:** 0.30 g **Cholesterol:** 0.00 mg **Sodium:** 218.61 mg **Sugars:** 0.30 g **Fiber:** 2.46 g

Easy and Delicious Spinach Dip

This dip is great with fresh vegetables sticks or whole wheat pita—a party favorite!

GBP: Weeks 4–6 Postop

BAND: Weeks 4–6 Postop

BPD: Weeks 4–6 Postop

INGREDIENTS

- 1 package (10 ounces, or 280 g) frozen, chopped spinach
- $1/2$ cup (50 g) chopped green onion
- $1/4$ teaspoon garlic powder
- 2 tablespoons (20 g) finely chopped red bell pepper
- $1/4$ cup (50 g) water chestnuts, drained and chopped
- 1 cup (200 g) nonfat sour cream
- 1 cup (230 g) nonfat mayonnaise
- 1 tablespoon (14 ml) lemon juice
- $1/2$ teaspoon salt
- $1/4$ teaspoon black pepper, ground

Thaw and drain the spinach in a colander, pressing all of the excess moisture out.

In a medium mixing bowl, mix the onion, garlic powder, bell pepper, water chestnuts, sour cream, mayonnaise, lemon juice, salt, and black pepper until well incorporated.

YIELD: Makes 14 (about $1/4$-cup) servings.

NUTRITIONAL ANALYSIS

Each with: **Calories:** 41.66 **Protein:** 1.85 g **Carbs:** 7.78 g **Total Fat:** 0.10 g **Sat Fat:** 0.01 g **Cholesterol:** 2.86 mg **Sodium:** 250.37 mg **Sugars:** 2.82 g **Fiber:** 0.79 g

Pacific Dungeness Crab Cakes

These crab cakes contain no bread or flour fillers, just pure, delicious Dungeness crab!

GBP: Weeks 4–6 Postop

BAND: Weeks 4–6 Postop

BPD: Weeks 4–6 Postop

INGREDIENTS

- $^1/_2$ pound (225 g) Dungeness crabmeat, cooked (any cooked crabmeat may be substituted, except for canned)
- 1 tablespoon (16 g) minced celery
- 2 teaspoons minced red bell pepper
- 2 teaspoons finely chopped fresh cilantro
- 2 tablespoons (30 g) nonfat mayonnaise
- $^1/_8$ teaspoon sea salt or kosher salt
- $^1/_8$ teaspoon cayenne pepper (optional)
- 2 teaspoons olive oil
- $^1/_2$ teaspoon toasted sesame oil
- 2 tablespoons (2 g) gourmet salad greens
- 2 lemon wedges
- 2 tablespoons (30 g) low-fat tartar sauce

NOTE

Two crab cakes equal the portion recommendation for an entrée serving, or one crab cake can be served as an appetizer. A little goes a long way with crabmeat, as it has a very rich flavor and texture.

Place the crabmeat in a strainer or colander and press out excess moisture.

Transfer the crabmeat to a medium mixing bowl, and add the celery, bell pepper, and cilantro.

In a small bowl, combine the mayonnaise, salt, and cayenne pepper (if using) and stir to mix.

Add the mayonnaise mixture to the crabmeat and mix until well incorporated.

Form the mixture into 6 equal patties (about 2 ounces, or 55 g each), pressing firmly enough to hold together, and place on waxed paper on top of a plate. Cover the top of the crab cakes with another sheet of waxed paper and refrigerate for 15 minutes.

In a medium, nonstick skillet, heat the olive oil and sesame oil over medium-high heat and swirl the pan to mix the oils. Gently place the crab cakes in the pan using a thin metal spatula and cook undisturbed for about 6 minutes on each side, until well browned, manipulating them only to avoid burning, then remove the pan from heat.

Place 1 tablespoon (1 g) of the greens in a pile on the center of a plate and place the crab cakes on the pile, leaning off of one side. Place a lemon wedge beside the greens and crab cakes and a teaspoon of the tartar sauce atop each cake.

YIELD: Makes 6 (about $1^1/_2$-ounces) crab cakes.

NUTRITIONAL ANALYSIS

Each with: **Calories:** 70.57 **Protein:** 8.49 g **Carbs:** 2.43 g **Total Fat:** 2.68 g **Sat Fat:** 0.29 g **Cholesterol:** 28.73 mg **Sodium:** 269.31 mg **Sugars:** 1.32 g **Fiber:** 0.12 g

Plum Tomatoes with Blue Cheese

This recipe is great as an appetizer for dinner parties. You could substitute feta cheese for the blue cheese and nonfat plain yogurt for the milk.

GBP: Weeks 6–8 Postop

BAND: Weeks 6–8 Postop

BPD: Weeks 6–8 Postop

INGREDIENTS

- 2 tablespoons (15 g) blue cheese
- 1 tablespoon (14 ml) nonfat milk
- $\frac{1}{2}$ teaspoon hot pepper sauce
- 12 medium Italian plum tomatoes, cored and cut in half lengthwise
- 1 tablespoon (4 g) chopped fresh parsley

In a medium mixing bowl, combine the cheese, milk, and pepper sauce, stirring vigorously to mix. Transfer to a small container, cover, and refrigerate for at least 30 minutes.

Top each tomato half equally with the cheese mixture and sprinkle evenly with parsley. Serve at room temperature.

YIELD: Makes 12 servings.

NUTRITIONAL ANALYSIS
Each with: **Calories:** 29.00 **Protein:** 1.64 g **Carbs:** 2.70 g **Total Fat:** 1.51 g **Sat Fat:** 0.91 g **Cholesterol:** 3.57 mg **Sodium:** 69.93 mg **Sugars:** 1.72 g **Fiber:** 0.80 g

Stuffed Mushrooms

This is another can't miss party favorite or dinner party appetizer and a great source of potassium.

GBP: Weeks 6–8 Postop

BAND: Weeks 6–8 Postop

BPD: Weeks 6–8 Postop

INGREDIENTS

- 1 pound (455 g) medium mushrooms (about 18)
- 1 tablespoon (14 ml) olive oil
- 1 clove garlic, minced
- 6 teaspoons finely diced red bell pepper
- 1/4 cup (40 g) finely diced yellow onion
- 2 tablespoons (15 g) thinly sliced green onion (green and white parts)
- 1 tablespoon (4 g) chopped fresh parsley
- 1/4 teaspoon dried basil
- 1/4 teaspoon dried oregano
- 3/4 cup (75 g) whole-wheat bread crumbs (about 1 1/2 slices bread, toasted)
- 2 tablespoons (10 g) grated Parmesan cheese

Preheat the oven to 375°F (190°C, or gas mark 5).

Clean the mushrooms and remove the stems. Finely chop or mince the stems and set aside.

Place the mushroom caps in a 9- x 13-inch (22.5- x 32.5-cm) baking dish.

In a medium nonstick skillet, heat the oil over medium-high heat. Add the mushroom stems and garlic and sauté for about 3 minutes. Add the bell pepper, yellow onion, green onion, parsley, basil, and oregano and continue cooking for about 4 minutes, until the peppers are soft. Remove from heat and add the bread crumbs and cheese. Stir to combine. Fill the mushroom caps with the stuffing mixture and bake for 20 minutes, until the mushrooms are soft.

YIELD: Makes 6 (about 1/2-cup) servings.

NUTRITIONAL ANALYSIS

Each with: **Calories:** 75.68 **Protein:** 4.14 g **Carbs:** 7.26 g **Total Fat:** 3.63 g **Sat Fat:** 0.87 g **Cholesterol:** 1.00 mg **Sodium:** 81.86 mg **Sugars:** 2.50 g **Fiber:** 1.59 g

Traditional Hummus

Serve this with cucumber slices, tomato wedges, Greek olives, and pita bread. Note that five Greek olives equals one serving of fat.

GBP: Weeks 4–6 Postop

BAND: Weeks 4–6 Postop

BPD: Weeks 3–6 Postop

INGREDIENTS

- 3–5 cloves fresh garlic, crushed
- 1 1/2 tablespoons (21 ml) extra-virgin olive oil, divided
- 3 cans (15 ounces, or 430 g each) cooked chickpeas (garbanzo beans), rinsed and drained
- 1/4 cup (60 g) sesame tahini
- 1/2 teaspoon toasted sesame oil
- 2 tablespoons (28 ml) cold water
- 2 tablespoons (28 ml) fresh lemon juice
- 1/2 teaspoon salt
- 2 teaspoons ground cumin

Place the garlic in a food processor with 1 1/2 teaspoons of the olive oil and process until the garlic is minced, almost paste-like. (You will need to stop the process and scrape down the garlic from the sides of the container a few times.) Add the chickpeas, tahini, sesame oil, water, lemon juice, salt, and cumin, and continue processing. While the puree is still processing, slowly add the remaining olive oil. (The consistency should have a smooth, but grainy texture. If a thinner consistency is preferred, add additional water in small increments.)

YIELD: Makes 16 (about 1/4-cup) servings.

NUTRITIONAL ANALYSIS:
Calories: 111.99 **Protein:** 4.74 g **Carbs:** 13.54 g **Total Fat:** 4.68 g **Sat Fat:** 0.59 g **Cholesterol:** 0.00 mg **Sodium:** 39.90 mg **Sugars:** 2.35 g **Fiber:** 3.89 g

Creamy Polenta with Fresh Oregano and Feta Cheese

Polenta is as versatile as it is easy and delicious. It can be served as a side dish, and it also stands on its own as an entrée when paired with your favorite tomato sauce. Try some of the variations listed (right).

GBP: Weeks 4–6 Postop

BAND: Weeks 4–6 Postop

BPD: Weeks 3–6 Postop

INGREDIENTS

- 1 cup (140 g) dry polenta meal (not corn meal)
- 1 cup (235 ml) nonfat milk
- 2¹⁄₂ cups (570 ml) water
- ¹⁄₈ teaspoon salt
- 2 tablespoons (8 g) chopped fresh oregano leaves
- ¹⁄₃ cup (50 g) feta cheese crumbles

Spray an 8- or 9-inch (20- or 22.5-cm) pie pan, a 7- x 7-inch (17.5- x 17.5-cm) baking dish, or sheet pan with cooking spray.

In a small bowl, place the polenta and pour the milk over the top. Stir the mixture to expose all the polenta to the liquid. (This process will eliminate lumps in the finished product.)

In a 1¹⁄₂-quart (1.5-L) saucepan, bring the water and salt to a soft boil and slowly add the soaked polenta, stirring constantly. Continue cooking, stirring, until the polenta begins to pull away from the sides of the pan. Remove the pan from the heat and stir in the oregano and cheese.

Immediately pour the polenta into the prepared pie pan or baking dish or spoon it free-form into a mound in the center of the sheet pan. Allow the polenta to cool until it sets enough to cut into squares or wedges (if serving from the free-form) and lifts away from the pan in one piece.

YIELD: Makes 8 (about ¹⁄₂-cup) servings.

NUTRITIONAL ANALYSIS
Each with: **Calories:** 125.51 **Protein:** 4.42 g **Carbs:** 23.82 g **Total Fat:** 1.46 g **Sat Fat:** 0.99 g **Cholesterol:** 6.18 mg **Sodium:** 104.50 mg **Sugars:** 1.77 g **Fiber:** 1.12 g

Variations

In place of water, use low-sodium chicken broth. In place of oregano and feta cheese, use ¹⁄₄ cup (25 g) chopped green onion and ¹⁄₃ cup (40 g) reduced-fat, shredded Cheddar cheese, or ¹⁄₄ cup (4 g) chopped fresh cilantro and 2 tablespoons (28 ml) lime juice, or 2 tablespoons (12 g) chopped green chilies and ¹⁄₃ cup (40 g) reduced-fat shredded Cheddar cheese. Or add 1 tablespoon (5 g) shredded Parmesan cheese.

Steamed Asparagus Lemonata

Pure and simple, this is a wonderful complement to meat, fish, poultry, or vegetarian entrées.

GBP: Weeks 6–8 Postop

BAND: Weeks 6–8 Postop

BPD: Weeks 6–8 Postop

INGREDIENTS

- 2$\frac{1}{2}$ cups (570 ml) water
- 1$\frac{3}{4}$ pounds (795 g) fresh "pencil" asparagus
- 1 tablespoon (14 ml) extra-virgin olive oil
- 1 teaspoon light butter
- 2 teaspoons fresh lemon juice
- 1 teaspoon lemon zest
- 1 teaspoon sea salt or kosher salt
- $\frac{1}{8}$ teaspoon ground white pepper
- $\frac{1}{8}$ teaspoon fresh cracked black pepper
- 2 teaspoons finely chopped fresh parsley

In a 2$\frac{1}{2}$-quart (2.5-L) saucepan with a steamer basket, bring the water to a boil.

Meanwhile, wash the asparagus and cut the wood-like ends off and discard. Place the prepared asparagus in the steamer basket and steam for 8 to 10 minutes, until the asparagus turns bright green and is fork-tender just below the tips.

While the asparagus is steaming, in a small saucepan, heat the oil, light butter, lemon juice, lemon zest, salt, white pepper, and black pepper, just until the lemon zest begins to bubble. Add the parsley at the last minute and stir.

Remove the asparagus from the steamer basket and place on a serving dish. Drizzle the oil and lemon mixture evenly over the asparagus and gently rotate for even exposure. Serve immediately.

YIELD: Makes 6 (about $\frac{1}{2}$-cup) servings.

NUTRITIONAL ANALYSIS
Each with: **Calories:** 51.77 **Protein:** 2.94 g **Carbs:** 5.37 g **Total Fat:** 2.83 g **Sat Fat:** 0.46 g **Cholesterol:** 0.00 mg **Sodium:** 86.24 mg **Sugars:** 2.54 g **Fiber:** 2.82 g

Mandarin Orange Broccoli

This Asian-influenced dish is fast, easy, and packed with satisfying flavors.

GBP: Weeks 6–8 Postop

BAND: Weeks 6–8 Postop

BPD: Weeks 6–8 Postop

INGREDIENTS

- 2 cans (11 ounces, or 310 g each) mandarin orange pieces, drained and liquid reserved
- 1 tablespoon (14 ml) molasses
- 1 tablespoon (14 ml) sugar-free maple syrup
- 1 tablespoon (14 ml) soy sauce
- 1 teaspoon fresh grated gingerroot
- 1 1/2 teaspoons cornstarch
- 1 teaspoon rice vinegar
- 1 tablespoon (14 ml) peanut oil
- 1 teaspoon sesame oil
- 2 heads fresh broccoli, cut into florets (5–6 cups, or 350–420 g)
- 2 tablespoons (15 g) toasted sesame seeds

In a small mixing bowl, mix together 1/4 cup (60 ml) of the reserved mandarin orange liquid and the molasses, maple syrup, soy sauce, gingerroot, cornstarch, and vinegar and set aside.

In a wok, heat the peanut oil and sesame oil over medium-high heat. Add the broccoli and one can of the mandarin oranges and cook, stirring briskly, until the broccoli is heated through. (The oranges will almost dissolve.) Stir in the soy-molasses mixture and continue to cook, while stirring the broccoli to coat, for about 3 minutes, until the broccoli is just tender. Remove from the heat and transfer to a serving dish. Sprinkle with the remaining mandarin orange pieces and toasted sesame seeds and serve immediately.

YIELD: Makes 8 (about 1/2-cup) servings.

NUTRITIONAL ANALYSIS

Each with: **Calories:** 128.60 **Protein:** 2.85 g **Carbs:** 17.38 g **Total Fat:** 5.93 g **Sat Fat:** 0.84 g **Cholesterol:** 0.00 mg **Sodium:** 88.94 mg **Sugars:** 12.13 g **Fiber:** 1.78 g

Edamame

Edamame, whole soybeans in the shell, is a simple and nutritious way to get more soy protein in your diet. Pop the shells open and eat the beans inside. You can find them fresh or frozen at your grocer.

GBP: Weeks 6–8 Postop

BAND: Weeks 6–8 Postop

BPD: Weeks 6–8 Postop

INGREDIENTS

- 2 1/2 quarts (2.5 L) water
- 1 tablespoon (18 g) salt
- 2 pounds (1 kg) fresh or frozen edamame
- 1/8 teaspoon coarse sea salt

In a 3-quart (3-L) pot, bring the water and table salt to a boil over high heat. Add the edamame, reduce the heat, and simmer for 3 minutes if using fresh beans or 4 minutes if using frozen.

Drain the beans and transfer them to a serving bowl just large enough to hold the edamame. (If the serving container is too large, the beans will cool off too quickly.) Toss the beans with the coarse sea salt and serve immediately.

YIELD: Makes 14 (about 1-cup) servings.

NUTRITIONAL ANALYSIS
Each with: **Calories:** 91.48 **Protein:** 7.62 g **Carbs:** 6.86 g **Total Fat:** 3.81 g **Sat Fat:** 0.38 g **Cholesterol:** 0.00 mg **Sodium:** 29.85 mg **Sugars:** 2.29 g **Fiber:** 3.05 g

Herb and Cheese
Mashed Cauliflower

Try this delicious and unique variation of cauliflower the whole family is sure to love.

GBP: Weeks 4-6 Postop

BAND: Weeks 4-6 Postop

BPD: Weeks 3-6 Postop

INGREDIENTS

- 2 1/2 cups (570 ml) water
- 3 cups (450 g) cauliflower florets (about 1-inch, or 2.5-cm pieces)
- 2/3 cup (155 ml) nonfat milk
- 1/4 cup (50 g) nonfat sour cream
- 1/2 teaspoon salt
- 1/8 teaspoon ground white pepper
- 2 tablespoons (15 g) finely chopped green onion
- 1 tablespoon (4 g) finely chopped fresh parsley
- 1 tablespoon (14 g) butter substitute

In a 2 1/2-quart (2.5-L) saucepan with a steamer basket, bring the water to a boil. Place the cauliflower in the steamer basket and steam for about 15 minutes, until the cauliflower is very tender throughout.

Place the cauliflower in a food processor fitted with a metal S blade and puree until smooth.

Add the milk and sour cream and carefully pulse the mixture until smooth. (Pulsate the mixture briefly to avoid the liquids splashing out of the processing bowl.) Add the salt, white pepper, onion, parsley, and butter substitute and continue pulsating until evenly incorporated. Serve warm as a side dish.

YIELD: Makes 4 (about 1-cup) servings.

NUTRITIONAL ANALYSIS
Each with: **Calories:** 88.13 **Protein:** 5.85 g **Carbs:** 14.28 g **Total Fat:** 1.76 g **Sat Fat:** 0.35 g **Cholesterol:** 3.32 mg **Sodium:** 251.67 mg **Sugars:** 7.13 g **Fiber:** 4.41 g

Boiled New Potatoes with Fresh Parsley

Pure, unadulterated deliciousness—this is a wonderful complement to roasted meat dishes.

GBP: Weeks 6–8 Postop

BAND: Weeks 6–8 Postop

BPD: Weeks 6–8 Postop

INGREDIENTS

- 1 pound (455 g) baby red potatoes, washed and halved
- 1 tablespoon (14 g) butter substitute
- $1/4$ teaspoon kosher salt
- $1/4$ teaspoon fresh cracked pepper
- $1/2$ teaspoon fresh lemon juice
- 2 tablespoons (8 g) chopped fresh parsley

In a 2-quart (2-L) saucepan, place the potatoes and enough cold water to cover 1 inch (2.5 cm) above the level of the potatoes. Bring the water to a boil and cook for about 12 minutes, until the potatoes can be gently speared with a fork when tested. Drain the potatoes in a colander and transfer them to a medium mixing bowl. While the potatoes are still hot, add the butter substitute, salt, pepper, lemon juice, and parsley. Gently toss the potatoes to evenly cover with all ingredients. Serve immediately.

YIELD: Makes 4 (about 1/2-cup) servings.

NUTRITIONAL ANALYSIS
Each with: **Calories:** 95.42 **Protein:** 2.23 g **Carbs:** 18.28 g **Total Fat:** 1.67 g **Sat Fat:** 0.28 g **Cholesterol:** 0.00 mg **Sodium:** 147.87 mg **Sugars:** 1.17 g **Fiber:** 2.02 g

Sweet Potatoes au Gratin

GBP: Weeks 4-6 Postop

BAND: Weeks 4-6 Postop

BPD: Weeks 3-6 Postop

INGREDIENTS

- 1 tablespoon (14 g) light butter
- 1 medium onion, finely diced
- 1 small clove fresh garlic, minced
- 2 1/2 cups (570 ml) low-sodium vegetable broth
- 1/2 cup (50 g) green onions, finely chopped
- 1/4 cup (15 g) chopped fresh parsley
- 1 cup (235 ml) nonfat milk
- 1/4 teaspoon salt
- 1/8 teaspoon ground black pepper
- 3 medium sweet potatoes, peeled and thinly sliced (about 2 1/2 pounds, 1.25 kg)
- 1/2 cup (55 g) shredded reduced-fat Cheddar cheese
- 1/4 cup (20 g) shredded Parmesan cheese

Preheat the oven to 375°F (190°C, or gas mark 5). Coat a 9- x 13-inch (22.5- x 32.5-cm) baking dish with cooking spray.

In a 2-quart (2-L) saucepan, melt the butter substitute over medium heat. Add the onion and garlic and sauté until the onion begins to soften, about 5 minutes. Add the broth, green onion, parsley, milk, salt, and pepper and bring to a simmer. Cook until the liquid is reduced to about 2¾ cups (650 ml). Add the sweet potatoes and return to a simmer. Continue cooking for an additional 5 minutes.

Pour the mixture into the prepared baking dish and bake for about 35 minutes, until the potatoes are tender, basting the potatoes occasionally with the liquid in the dish. Top the dish evenly with the Cheddar and then the Parmesan and continue to bake for about 20 minutes, until the cheese is bubbly and golden brown.

YIELD: Makes 16 (about ¾-cup) servings.

NUTRITIONAL ANALYSIS

Each with: **Calories:** 104.14 **Protein:** 3.96 g **Carbs:** 17.54 g **Total Fat:** 2.03 g **Sat Fat:** 1.03 g **Cholesterol:** 4.37 mg **Sodium:** 116.62 mg **Sugars:** 4.09 g **Fiber:** 2.15 g

Citrus-Roasted Carrots with Honey

This is a wonderful accompaniment to fish and poultry.

GBP: Weeks 6–8 Postop

BAND: Weeks 6–8 Postop

BPD: Weeks 6–8 Postop

INGREDIENTS

- 1 tablespoon (14 ml) olive oil
- 2 teaspoons light butter
- Juice of $\frac{1}{2}$ lemon
- 1 teaspoon honey
- $\frac{1}{8}$ teaspoon sea salt or kosher salt
- $\frac{1}{8}$ teaspoon ground white pepper
- 1 pound (455 g) baby carrots, peeled
- 1 tablespoon (4 g) chopped fresh parsley

Preheat the oven to 375°F (190°C, or gas mark 5). Spray a 7- x 9-inch (17.5- x 22.5-cm) baking dish with cooking spray.

In a medium skillet, heat the oil, butter, lemon juice, honey, salt, and pepper over medium heat. Add the carrots and turn until coated with the mixture.

Transfer mixture to the prepared baking dish. Roast on the medium rack for 20 to 30 minutes, until the carrots are tender and caramelized.

YIELD: Makes 6 (about $\frac{1}{2}$-cup) servings.

NUTRITIONAL ANALYSIS

Each with: **Calories:** 59.93 **Protein:** 0.55 g **Carbs:** 8.07 g **Total Fat:** 3.11 g **Sat Fat:** 0.46 g **Cholesterol:** 0.00 mg **Sodium:** 93.39 mg **Sugars:** 4.74 g **Fiber:** 1.44 g

CHAPTER 8
Dry Rubs for Meats and Poultry

Use dry rubs to add a dynamic flare to meats, fish, poultry, or slices of fresh drained tofu. This is a wonderful way to pack in the flavor. An additional benefit of using dry rubs is that the acids in certain spices will begin to chemically "cook" the product before heat is applied, rendering meats more tender than you might expect. Dry rubs work especially well when cooking on the grill.

Try any of our recommended dry rubs using the following guide: Work the spice mix well into the product, covering entirely. Next, simply let the meat, fish, or poultry stand covered in the refrigerator. Let red meats and pork stand for at least 2 hours, poultry for at least 1 hour, and lighter-textured products such as fish or tofu for at least 30 minutes.

Dill Rub

GBP: Weeks 2–4 Postop

BAND: Weeks 2–4 Postop

BPD: Weeks 2–4 Postop

INGREDIENTS

- 2 tablespoons (18 g) onion powder
- 1 teaspoon garlic powder
- 1 tablespoon (2 g) ground sage
- ¹/₂ teaspoon nutmeg
- 1 teaspoon dry mustard
- 2 teaspoons salt-free lemon-pepper seasoning

In a small bowl, combine all of the ingredients.

YIELD: Enough rub for 3 to 4 pounds (1.5 to 2 kg) of chicken or a 5-pound (2.5-kg) roasting hen.

NUTRITIONAL ANALYSIS
Total recipe: **Calories:** 106.65 **Protein:** 3.51 g **Carbs:** 17.77 g **Total Fat:** 2.64 g **Sat Fat:** 0.46 g **Cholesterol:** 0.00 mg **Sodium:** 13.91 mg **Sugars:** 6.14 g **Fiber:** 2.27 g

Pork Roast Rub

GBP: Weeks 2–4 Postop

BAND: Weeks 2–4 Postop

BPD: Weeks 2–4 Postop

INGREDIENTS

- 1 tablespoon (9 g) onion powder
- 2 teaspoons garlic powder
- 2 teaspoons paprika
- 2 teaspoons oregano
- 2 teaspoons ground thyme
- ¹/₈ teaspoon cayenne pepper
- ¹/₈ teaspoon black pepper
- ¹/₂ teaspoon salt

In a small bowl, combine all of the ingredients.

YIELD: Enough rub for a 2- to 3-pound (1- to 1.5-kg) pork loin roast.

NUTRITIONAL ANALYSIS
Total recipe: **Calories:** 65.43 **Protein:** 2.68 g **Carbs:** 14.19 g **Total Fat:** 0.93 g **Sat Fat:** 0.17 g **Cholesterol:** 0.00 mg **Sodium:** 582.34 mg **Sugars:** 4.43 g **Fiber:** 3.73 g

Cajun Blackened Rub

GBP: Weeks 2–4 Postop

BAND: Weeks 2–4 Postop

BPD: Weeks 2–4 Postop

INGREDIENTS

- 2 teaspoons ground oregano
- 1 teaspoon ground thyme
- $^1/_2$ teaspoon cayenne pepper
- $^1/_2$ teaspoon ground black pepper
- $^1/_2$ teaspoon ground white pepper
- 1 teaspoon garlic powder
- 1 teaspoon onion powder

In a small bowl, combine all of the ingredients.

YIELD: Enough rub for a 2- pound (1-kg) chicken.

NUTRITIONAL ANALYSIS

Total recipe: **Calories:** 69.19 **Protein:** 3.03 g **Carbs:** 13.41 g
Total Fat: 1.66 g **Sat Fat:** 0.22 g **Cholesterol:** 0.00 mg **Sodium:**
7.87 mg **Sugars:** 2.51 g **Fiber:** 5.22 g

Dry Jamaican Jerk Rub

GBP: Weeks 2–4 Postop

BAND: Weeks 2–4 Postop

BPD: Weeks 2–4 Postop

INGREDIENTS

- 1 tablespoon (9 g) onion powder
- 1 teaspoon ground thyme
- 2 teaspoons brown sugar
- 2 teaspoons dried chives
- 1 teaspoon salt
- 2 teaspoons allspice
- 1 teaspoon ground black pepper
- $^1/_2$ teaspoon ground celery seed

In a small bowl, combine all of the ingredients.

YIELD: Enough rub for $1^1/_2$ pounds (700 g) white
fish or a 1-pound (455 g) chicken.

NUTRITIONAL ANALYSIS

Total recipe: **Calories:** 79.69 **Protein:** 1.61 g **Carbs:** 18.49 g
Total Fat: 0.67 g **Sat Fat:** 0.16 g **Cholesterol:** 0.00 mg
Sodium: 1158.89 mg **Sugars:** 10.56 g **Fiber:**
1.89 g

Whole Roasted Chicken
with Potatoes and Brussels Sprouts

This dinner is easy and elegant, yet packed with flavor from the garlic and white wine.

GBP: Weeks 6–8 Postop

BAND: Weeks 6–8 Postop

BPD: Weeks 6–8 Postop

INGREDIENTS

- 1 (5-pound, or 2.5-kg) whole chicken
- 2 teaspoons sea salt or kosher salt
- 1/2 teaspoon black pepper
- 1 teaspoon dried basil
- 4 cloves fresh garlic, halved
- 1/2 cup (120 ml) white wine or chicken stock
- 2 cups (475 ml) water
- 2 tablespoons (28 ml) lemon juice (about 1/2 lemon)
- 12 small to medium baby red potatoes, washed and halved
- 18 Brussels sprouts, washed, trimmed, and halved
- Fresh sprigs parsley

Preheat the oven to 400°F (200°C, or gas mark 6).

Remove all innards from the chicken. Using kitchen shears or a filet knife, remove all of the skin and trim all of the excess fat.

In a small cup or bowl, combine the salt, pepper, and basil and mix well into a dry rub.

Rub the seasonings evenly on all surface areas of the chicken. Place the chicken breast side down in a 6-quart (6-L) roasting pan with a lid. Add the garlic, wine or stock, water, and lemon juice to the pan. Place the potatoes on one side of the pan, and the Brussels sprouts on the other, along with the chicken.

Cover with the lid and bake for about 1 hour and 15 minutes, basting with the liquid in the pan three or four times. Remove the cover and continue baking for an additional 30 minutes, until a leg can easily be separated from the body when checked with a fork, and the juices from the chicken run clear. (If using a meat thermometer, the internal temperature of the breast should be about 180°F.) Remove the chicken from the pan and let stand for about 5 minutes before carving. For an elegant presentation, serve the chicken, potatoes, and Brussels sprouts on the same serving platter, decorated with fresh parsley sprigs.

"I loved this. It was great to take to work the next day."

—Heather,
a gastric bypass surgery patient in the Boston area

YIELD: Makes 6 (about 3-4 ounces chicken, 6 Brussels sprout halves, and 4 potato halves) servings.

NUTRITIONAL ANALYSIS

Each with: **Calories:** 356.93 **Protein:** 29.41 g **Carbs:** 45.76 g **Total Fat:** 4.89 g **Sat Fat:** 0.16 g **Cholesterol:** 76.00 mg **Sugars:** 3.54 g **Sodium:** 464.20 mg

MARGARET'S NOTE

A 5-pound (2.5-kg) chicken will yield approximately 16 ounces (455 g) of white meat and 8 ounces (225 g) of dark meat. The white meat of chicken is lower in fat and cholesterol than the dark meat. You might want to add fat-free gravy or another type of low-fat sauce to make sure it's as moist as possible. The dark meat, with the skin removed, is Okay in moderation (about 3 ounces, 85 g. a few times a week), but it's important to avoid the skin to keep the saturated fat and cholesterol down.

Curried Pork Loin Roast
with Currants, Apples, and Sweet Onions

Begin this a day ahead of time for maximum flavor. The dry rub is also delicious for chicken or beef.
Creamy Polenta (the plain with Parmesan cheese version on page 150) makes a lovely accompaniment to
this roast. Add Steamed Asparagus Lemonata (page 158) for a complete menu and finish European style
with Watercress Salad with Tarragon and Mint Leaves (page 124), for a four-course extravaganza!

GBP: Weeks 6–8 Postop

BAND: Weeks 6–8 Postop

BPD: Weeks 6–8 Postop

INGREDIENTS

- 1¹/₂-pound (700 g) pork tenderloin roast
- 1 teaspoon kosher salt
- ¹/₄ teaspoon ground white pepper
- 1 tablespoon (7 g) curry powder
- ¹/₂ teaspoon ground cumin
- ¹/₄ teaspoon cinnamon
- ¹/₄ teaspoon cayenne pepper
- ¹/₈ teaspoon cracked black pepper
- 2 teaspoons olive oil
- 1 teaspoon butter substitute
- 1¹/₂ cups (240 g) diced sweet onion
- 3 tablespoons (20 g) black currants
- ¹/₄ cup (40 g) skinned, cored, and diced green apple
- ¹/₂ cup (120 ml) white wine for cooking or chicken broth

Trim the roast of all excess fat. Place the roast on a piece of parchment or waxed paper.

In a small bowl, combine the salt, white pepper, curry powder, cumin, cinnamon, cayenne pepper, and black pepper and mix together. Distribute the dry rub evenly over the roast and rub it well into the entire surface. Wrap the roast tightly in the parchment or waxed paper, place it in a dish, cover it, and cure it overnight in the refrigerator.

Remove the roast from the refrigerator 20 minutes prior to cooking.

Preheat the oven to 375°F (190°C, or gas mark 5).

In a 7- or 8-inch (17.5- or 20-cm) skillet, heat the oil and butter over medium-high heat. Brown the roast on all sides and place it in a 3-quart (3-L) roasting pan with a lid.

In the same skillet, place the onions, currants, and apple and sauté for 3 to 4 minutes, stirring often to release any brown bits from the bottom of the pan. Add the wine or broth and scrape the bottom of the skillet, incorporating all of the ingredients and absorbing the flavor of the brown bits into the sauté. Continue this process for 1 minute. Pour the sauté mixture over the roast, cover, and bake the roast for 50 to 60 minutes. Uncover and let rest for 10 minutes before carving. Serve the roast on a platter, sliced diagonally, with the onion, apple, and currant mixture over the top.

YIELD: Makes 8 (3-ounce) servings.

NUTRITIONAL ANALYSIS
Each with: **Calories:** 187.72 **Protein:** 24.24 g **Carbs:** 5.07 g **Total Fat:** 6.81 g **Sat Fat:** 2.06 g **Cholesterol:** 67.19 mg **Sodium:** 332.38 mg **Sugars:** 3.06 g **Fiber:** 1.07 g

MARGARET'S NOTE

As I mentioned in the Early Postoperative Nutrition Guide (Chapter 1), fresh cracked or fresh ground pepper can have a great deal more flavor compared to prepackaged ground pepper. Oil in the peppercorn dehydrates at a much faster rate after it is ground, and so the flavor dissipates as well. Truly fresh black pepper will have a fruity aroma and a hearty bite.

In addition, I find that it's worth researching where your spices come from. Dried spices and seasonings will lose the intensity of flavor as they age. Quality ingredients, including spices and seasonings, can contribute a world of difference to your recipes.

Lobster and Scallop Sauté
with Fresh Steamed Green Beans

GBP: Weeks 6–8 Postop

BAND: Weeks 6–8 Postop

BPD: Weeks 6–8 Postop

INGREDIENTS

- 1 slice reduced-calorie whole-wheat bread
- 1 cup (100 g) fresh green beans
- Small dash salt
- Small dash pepper
- 2 large sea scallops, sliced in half horizontally
- 2 teaspoons butter substitute
- ¼ cup (35 g) shelled lobster meat
- 2 tablespoons (28 ml) white wine

Toast the bread, cut it into small cubes, then season it with the salt and pepper.

In a microwave-safe bowl, place the green beans and cover them with water. Place a microwave-safe plate on top of the bowl. Steam the green beans for 4 minutes in the microwave

Coat a 6-inch (15-cm) nonstick omelet pan with cooking spray and heat over high heat. Sear the scallop halves on both sides, transfer to a bowl, and set aside. In the same pan, melt the butter substitute over medium-high heat. Add the lobster, scallops with any juices, and the wine. Cook for about 8 minutes, stirring occasionally, until the wine has reduced a bit and the lobster is cooked. (Lobster is cooked when all translucency has disappeared and the meat is solid white throughout.) Transfer the lobster and scallops to a serving plate or an entrée bowl, top with the croutons and garnish with green beans on one side.

YIELD: Makes about 2 servings

NUTRITIONAL ANALYSIS
Each with: **Calories:** 123.87 **Protein:** 13.24 g **Carbs:** 9.10 g **Total Fat:** 2.76 g **Sat Fat:** 0.43 g **Cholesterol:** 40.39 mg **Sodium:** 442.55 mg **Sugars:** 1.93 g **Fiber:** 2.89 g

Breaded Grouper Fillets

This is sinfully delicious and healthy, too.

GBP: Weeks 4–6 Postop

BAND: Weeks 4–6 Postop

BPD: Weeks 3–6 Postop

INGREDIENTS

- 2 tablespoons (30 g) light mayonnaise
- $1/4$ teaspoon lemon zest
- 2 teaspoons water
- 2 teaspoons lemon juice
- $1^1/2$ pounds (700 g) grouper fillets, cut into approximately 4-ounce (115 g) pieces
- 1 cup (100 g) seasoned bread crumbs
- 2 tablespoons (8 g) chopped fresh parsley
- 1 lemon, cut into 6 wedges

Preheat the oven to 375°F (190°C, or gas mark 5). Spray a baking sheet with cooking spray.

In a shallow 2-quart (2-L) mixing bowl, combine the mayonnaise, lemon zest, water, and lemon juice. Place the fillets in the mixture and coat evenly.

Pour the bread crumbs onto a dinner plate. One at a time, lightly coat the fillets in the bread crumbs and place them on the prepared baking sheet. Bake for 15 minutes, until golden and crispy. Place the fillets on a serving plate, sprinkle with the parsley and garnish with the lemon.

YIELD: Makes 6 (3-ounce) servings.

NUTRITIONAL ANALYSIS
Each with: **Calories:** 198.51 **Protein:** 24.85 g **Carbs:** 14.27 g **Total Fat:** 3.93 g **Sat Fat:** 0.88 g **Cholesterol:** 43.82 mg **Sodium:** 445.97 mg **Sugars:** 1.20 g **Fiber:** 1.04 g

Fillet of Sole with Vegetables Baked in Parchment

So easy and virtually no mess to clean up, these vegetables require very little attention and are cooked to perfection as they steam with the fish in parchment paper.

GBP: Weeks 4–6 Postop

BAND: Weeks 4–6 Postop

BPD: Weeks 3–6 Postop

INGREDIENTS

- 4 (5-ounce, or 140 g) sole fillets
- 2 teaspoons olive oil
- 1/8 teaspoon salt
- 1/8 teaspoon ground pepper
- 4 thin lemon slices
- 2 tablespoons (8 g) chopped fresh parsley
- 12 asparagus spears
- 2 small summer squash, stems removed and cut in half, lengthwise

Preheat the oven to 375°F (190°C, or gas mark 5). Cut 4 sheets of parchment paper into 12- x 12-inch (30- x 30-cm) squares and fold each in half.

Open the sheets and place one fillet in the center of the sheet, just below the fold. Rub both sides of each fillet with just enough oil to give a shiny appearance, then sprinkle evenly with the salt and pepper. Place a lemon slice in the center of each fillet and evenly sprinkle with the parsley.

Trim the ends from the asparagus and discard, and then place 3 spears directly under each fillet.

Slice the squash into about 1/4-inch (6 mm) half circles and pile the pieces equally on top of the asparagus. Carefully fold the open three edges of the parchment together tightly, leaving room for air and steam to circulate around the contents of the packet. Staple the folds shut with 2 or 3 staples for each edge and place the 4 packets on a baking sheet. Bake for 15 to 20 minutes. Let stand for about 5 minutes before placing the packets on dinner plates. (You may wish to remove the contents from the parchment entirely before serving, or simply just leave it in the parchment for the individual to deconstruct. That's the fun part! Slice a small incision in the parchment with a small, sharp knife and tear the rest of the way open.)

YIELD: Makes 4 servings (about 4 oz sole, 3 asparagus spears, and 1/2 squash = 1 serving).

NUTRITIONAL ANALYSIS

Each with: **Calories:** 164.79 **Protein:** 26.23 g **Carbs:** 4.25 g **Total Fat:** 5.21 g **Sat Fat:** 0.81 g **Cholesterol:** 70.87 mg **Sodium:** 173.27 mg **Sugars:** 2.37 g **Fiber:** 1.87 g

Baked Sea Bass

This is as easy as it is delicious. Impress your friends with this recipe at your next dinner party.

GBP: Weeks 4-6 Postop

BAND: Weeks 4-6 Postop

BPD: Weeks 3-6 Postop

INGREDIENTS

- 1¼ pounds (570 g) sea bass
- ½ teaspoon sea salt or kosher salt
- ¼ teaspoon white pepper
- ¼ teaspoon black pepper
- 2 tablespoons (28 ml) extra-virgin olive oil
- 1 tablespoon (3 g) thinly sliced chives
- 2 tablespoons (28 ml) sherry wine for cooking or chicken broth
- 2 teaspoons fresh lemon juice

Cut the fillets into 4 equal servings and place them in a medium baking dish, skin sides down.

In a small bowl, combine the salt and white pepper and lightly coat both sides of the fillets. Sprinkle the top with the black pepper. Cover and let stand in refrigerator for 10 to 15 minutes.

In a small bowl, combine the oil, chives, sherry or broth, and lemon juice and briefly whisk with a fork or wire whisk. Spread the mixture evenly over the fillets and let stand for an additional 10 minutes.

Preheat the oven to 400°F (200°C, or gas mark 6) and bake the fillets about 7 minutes for every inch of thickness, until the center of the fillets are no longer translucent and the outsides of the fillets begin to flake when tested with a fork. Let the fillets stand and cool for about 3 minutes. With a metal spatula, remove the fillets by separating the flesh from the skin and place them in the center of a serving plate.

YIELD: Makes 4 (about 6-ounce) servings.

NUTRITIONAL ANALYSIS
Each with: **Calories:** 207.43 **Protein:** 26.33 g **Carbs:** 0.40 g **Total Fat:** 9.87 g **Sat Fat:** 1.73 g **Cholesterol:** 58.12 mg **Sodium:** 332.99 mg **Sugars:** 0.13 g **Fiber:** 0.14 g

LYNETTE'S NOTE

Colorful garnishes for this plate include fresh, edible flowers, such as nasturtiums, lemon wedges, or fresh herb sprigs.

Filet of Salmon à la Herman

We eat a lot of salmon here in the Pacific Northwest. Herman is my dad, and this was his favorite way to cook it. It also gave my mom a break from the kitchen once in a while! My dad used to soak a few small alder branches in a bucket of water for several hours beforehand, and then put them on the grill along with the salmon for that great Pacific Northwest alder smoke flavor.

GBP: Weeks 4–6 Postop

BAND: Weeks 4–6 Postop

BPD: Weeks 3–6 Postop

INGREDIENTS

- 1¹/₂ pounds (700 g) wild salmon fillet, cut into 6 (4-ounce, or 115 g) portions
- ¹/₄ teaspoon sea salt or kosher salt
- ¹/₂ lemon, juice and rind (no seeds)
- ¹/₄ cup (55 g) butter substitute
- ¹/₂ large yellow onion, diced
- 1 tablespoon (6 g) fresh cracked black pepper

LYNETTE'S NOTE

This salmon is served perfectly with a garden salad and any of our low-fat dressings on pages 126 to 129.

Prepare the charcoal or gas grill for medium-high heat. Make a "boat" for each of the salmon fillets using heavy aluminum foil by placing the fillet in the center and then folding the edges up around it. Evenly sprinkle the salt over the salmon fillets.

Squeeze the lemon into a small bowl and chop the rind (yellow and white part) into very small pieces, then set aside.

In a small saucepan, melt the butter substitute over medium-high heat. Add the chopped onion and cook until it begins to soften. Add the lemon juice and rind and continue to cook for about 2 minutes, stirring often. Add the pepper, cook for 1 more minute, and remove from the heat. Spoon the sauce over the salmon fillets and place the "boats" on the grill. Cook for about 7 minutes for every inch of thickness of the salmon fillets. When the juice from the salmon begins to appear opaque, it is a good indication of medium-well doneness.

YIELD: Makes 6 (about 4-ounce) servings.

NUTRITIONAL ANALYSIS
Each with: **Calories:** 207.43 **Protein:** 22.90 g **Carbs:** 3.06 g **Total Fat:** 11.21 g **Sat Fat:** 1.78 g **Cholesterol:** 62.37 mg **Sodium:** 204.51 mg **Sugars:** 0.98 g **Fiber:** 0.50 g

Grilled Salmon with Toasted Fennel and Paprika

GBP: Weeks 4-6 Postop

BAND: Weeks 4-6 Postop

BPD: Weeks 3-6 Postop

INGREDIENTS

- 1 tablespoon (6 g) fennel seeds
- 2 tablespoons (30 g) packed golden brown sugar
- 3 tablespoons (20 g) Spanish smoked paprika
- 1 tablespoon (19 g) coarse kosher salt
- 2 teaspoons freshly ground black pepper
- 2 teaspoons dried dill weed
- 3-pound (1.5 kg) side of salmon with skin (preferably wild salmon—see Lynette's note)
- 1 tablespoon (14 ml) olive oil
- Several whole fresh parsley sprigs (optional)

LYNETTE'S NOTE

When possible, choose wild salmon over farmed. Farmed salmon contains chemical dyes, antibiotics, growth hormones, and other toxins from being raised in concentrated numbers and unnaturally close proximity to other salmon in the net pens.

Preheat the oven to 350°F (180°C, or gas mark 4).

On a sheet pan, spread out the fennel seeds. Bake them in the oven for about 10 minutes, until the seeds are toasted. (You will smell them when they are done!) Remove the seeds from the oven and let cool. Finely grind the fennel seeds in a spice mill or coffee grinder, then transfer them to a small bowl. Add the sugar, paprika, salt, pepper, and dill weed.

Before lighting the grill, spray the rack with cooking spray. Prepare the barbecue grill for medium-high heat. Brush the salmon lightly on both sides with the oil. Rub the spice mixture generously over the flesh side of the salmon.

Place the salmon skin side down on a heavy-duty sheet of foil, folding the edges of the foil up to form a "boat" for the salmon. Place the "boat" on the grill.

Close the lid on the barbecue and grill for about 8 minutes, just until the juice from the sides of the fillet appears opaque. Open the lid on the grill and continue cooking for about an additional 5 minutes, just until the juice on the top of the fillet begins to appear opaque. (Opaque-colored juice on the top of the salmon indicates a "medium" temperature in the center.)

Remove the salmon from the grill and slide it onto a serving dish. Place the parsley (if using) around the fillet for a beautiful presentation.

YIELD: Makes 10 (about 3½-ounce) servings.

NUTRITIONAL ANALYSIS

Each with: **Calories:** 220.04 **Protein:** 27.57 g **Carbs:** 4.53 g **Total Fat:** 9.68 g **Sat Fat:** 1.48 g **Cholesterol:** 74.84 mg **Sodium:** 438.47 mg **Sugars:** 2.61 g **Fiber:** 1.06 g

MARGARET'S NOTE

Although this recipe is a bit higher in total fat (40 percent calories from fat compared with our usual limit of 30 percent of calories from fat), salmon is high in the "good" fats, like the omega-3-fatty acids and monounsaturated fats, with none of the bad "trans" fats and very little saturated fat, so it's a heart-healthy meal.

Slow-Cooked Bone-In White Chicken Chili

This dinner literally cooks on its own while you're away at work or play.

GBP: Weeks 4–6 Postop

BAND: Weeks 4–6 Postop

BPD: Weeks 3–6 Postop

INGREDIENTS

- 1 pound (455 g) skinless chicken thighs
- 1 pound (455 g) dry Great Northern White beans, rinsed (about 2$\frac{1}{2}$ cups)
- 6 cups (1410 ml) low-fat, low-sodium chicken broth
- 2 tablespoons (30 g) low-sodium tomato paste
- 1 medium green bell pepper, cored and diced (about $\frac{3}{4}$ cup, or 105 g)
- 1 large medium yellow onion, diced (about 1$\frac{1}{2}$ cups, or 240 g)
- 3–6 cloves fresh garlic, chopped
- 1 jalapeno pepper, seeded and minced (optional)
- 1 tablespoon (4 g) dried oregano
- 3 teaspoons ground cumin
- 2 teaspoons paprika
- 1 tablespoon (9 g) chili powder
- $\frac{1}{2}$ teaspoon cayenne pepper (optional)
- Fresh cilantro sprigs
- Nonfat sour cream

Rinse the chicken and pat them dry with paper towels.

Place the beans in the slow cooker, along with broth and tomato paste. Stir to dissolve the tomato paste and add the chicken, bell pepper, onion, garlic, jalapeno pepper, oregano, cumin, paprika, chili powder, and cayenne pepper (if using). Cook on high for 10 hours. Serve in warm bowls and top each with a sprig of cilantro and a teaspoon of sour cream.

YIELD: Makes 8 (about $\frac{3}{4}$-cup) servings.

NUTRITIONAL ANALYSIS
Each with: **Calories:** 269.78 **Protein:** 25.62 g **Carbs:** 32.44 g **Total Fat:** 3.68 g **Sat Fat:** 0.85 g **Cholesterol:** 47.06 mg **Sodium:** 111.86 mg **Sugars:** 4.37 g **Fiber:** 11.59 g

Maria and Karen's Zesty Lemon and Caper Chicken

Thanks, Maria and Karen, for creating this ultra-tasty dish.

GBP: Weeks 6–8 Postop

BAND: Weeks 6–8 Postop

BPD: Weeks 6–8 Postop

INGREDIENTS

- 1 pound (455 g) boneless chicken breasts cut in half, lengthwise
- ¹⁄₈ teaspoon salt
- ¹⁄₈ teaspoon black pepper
- 1 tablespoon (14 ml) olive oil
- 2 teaspoons light butter
- ¹⁄₄ cup (60 ml) low sodium, nonfat chicken broth
- ¹⁄₄ cup (60 ml) white wine or chicken broth
- 2 tablespoons (20 g) capers, rinsed
- Juice and zest of 1 lemon, (about ¹⁄₄ cup, or 60 ml juice)
- ¹⁄₄ teaspoon garlic powder
- Chopped fresh parsley

"My family and I loved this recipe, and it was really easy to make (and healthy too!). The chicken was very tender and had lots of flavor. We will definitely make this on a regular basis. Thanks so much!"

—Kim, *a gastric bypass surgery patient in the Boston area*

Rinse the chicken breasts and pat them dry with paper towels.

Sprinkle the salt and pepper on both sides of the chicken.

In a medium nonstick skillet, heat the oil and butter over medium-high heat. When the oil is hot, just before the butter begins to brown, add the chicken. Brown the chicken on both sides and remove the breasts from the pan and set aside, reserving all that remains in the bottom of the pan. (The chicken is not done in the middle at this point. It will finish cooking in the next phase of the recipe.) Add the wine or broth, capers, lemon juice, and garlic powder to the skillet and return it to a simmer, scraping the bottom of the pan to release all of the browned bits into the sauce. Simmer at least 2 to 3 minutes more, until the sauce is slightly reduced. Return the chicken breasts to the pan along with any exuded juices and cover with a lid. Continue cooking for about 5 minutes, until the chicken is done at its thickest portion.

Place the chicken breasts on a serving platter or onto dinner plates and pour equal amounts of the sauce over each one. For extra zest, grate a small amount of lemon peel (thin yellow skin only) onto the chicken just before serving. A sprinkle of chopped fresh parsley makes an additional and complementary tasting garnish.

YIELD: Makes 4 (about 3-ounce) servings.

NUTRITIONAL ANALYSIS

Each with: **Calories:** 180.02 **Protein:** 26.35 g **Carbs:** 1.61 g **Total Fat:** 5.91 g **Sat Fat:** 1.04 g **Cholesterol:** 65.77 mg **Sodium:** 371.15 mg **Sugars:** 0.48 g **Fiber:** 0.09 g

Boneless Chicken Breast Cacciatore

This easy and flavorful dish is sure to please your craving for Italian food.

GBP: Weeks 6–8 Postop

BAND: Weeks 6–8 Postop

BPD: Weeks 6–8 Postop

INGREDIENTS

- 1¹/₂ pounds (700 g) boneless, skinless chicken breasts (about six 4-ounce, 115 g chicken breasts)
- 1 teaspoon salt
- ¹/₂ teaspoon black pepper, ground
- 1 tablespoon (14 ml) extra-virgin olive oil
- 1¹/₂ large green bell peppers, seeded, membranes removed, and cut into ¹/₂-inch (1.25-cm) strips
- 1 cup (160 g) medium yellow onion, cut into ¹/₂-inch (1.25-cm) strips
- 1³/₄ cups (315 g) diced plum tomatoes or 1 can (14¹/₂ ounces, or 415 g), whole, no salt added, peeled tomatoes
- 2 tablespoons (30 g) low-sodium tomato paste
- 2 tablespoons (28 ml) lemon juice (¹/₂ fresh lemon)
- 1 teaspoon dried oregano
- 1 teaspoon dried basil
- 1 teaspoon dried thyme

Preheat the oven to 375°F (190°C, or gas mark 5). Spray a 9- x 13-inch (22.5- x 32.5-cm) glass baking dish with cooking spray.

Sprinkle both sides of the chicken with the salt and pepper.

Coat a 10-inch (25-cm) skillet with cooking spray. Heat the oil over medium-high heat. Place the chicken in the hot skillet, smoothest side down. Cook for about 4 minutes, until browned on one side only, then place the chicken browned side up into the prepared baking dish.

Return the skillet to the stove and add the peppers and onion. Cook over medium-high heat, until the edges begin to brown. Add the tomatoes, breaking them up slightly with your hands first, along with the juice. Add the tomato paste, lemon juice, oregano, basil, and thyme and then stir with a rubber spatula, loosening any brown bits in the bottom of the pan. Pour all of the mixture over the chicken and bake uncovered for 20 minutes, until the thickest portion of chicken is done. (The juice should run clear when tested in the middle. If using a meat thermometer, the internal temperature should be about 180°F.)

YIELD: Makes 6 (about 3-ounce) servings.

NUTRITIONAL ANALYSIS
Each with: **Calories:** 185.77 **Protein:** 28.23 g **Carbs:** 8.68 g **Total Fat:** 3.94 g **Sat Fat:** 0.74 g **Cholesterol:** 65.77 mg **Sodium:** 321.27 mg **Sugars:** 4.61 g **Fiber:** 2.13 g

"This is a great chicken dish when you are sick of chicken! There is just enough flair to it given by the peppers and onion. I added some fresh herbs that I had on hand and they were a wonderful addition. I also added some low-fat shredded mozzarella, and it made it almost like low-fat chicken Parmesan, only with very tangy sauce. This took almost no time to make and only two pans to clean up!"

—**Juli,** *a gastric bypass surgery patient in the New Bedford, Massachusetts, area*

Chicken, Broccoli, and Mushroom Casserole

This "almost one pot" casserole makes an easy and delicious dinner for the whole family.

GBP: Weeks 6–8 Postop

BAND: Weeks 6–8 Postop

BPD: Weeks 6–8 Postop

INGREDIENTS

- 6 (4-ounce, or 115 g) boneless, skinless chicken breasts
- 1/8 teaspoon salt
- 1/8 teaspoon black pepper
- 1 package (10 ounces, or 280 g) frozen broccoli florets
- 2 teaspoons light butter
- 3/4 pound (340 g) fresh mushrooms, cleaned and sliced
- 1 can (8 ounces, or 225 g) low-fat condensed cream of celery soup
- 2 teaspoons lemon juice
- 1/2 cup (120 ml) nonfat milk
- 1/4 cup (25 g) sliced green onions (white and green parts)
- 1/4 cup (25 g) seasoned bread crumbs
- 2 tablespoons (10 g) grated Parmesan cheese
- 2 tablespoons (8 g) finely chopped fresh parsley

Preheat the oven to 375°F (190°C, or gas mark 5). Spray a medium-large (about 9- x 13-inch, or 22.5- x 32.5-cm) baking dish with cooking spray.

Sprinkle the chicken with the salt and pepper and place them in the prepared baking dish. Bake the chicken for 15 minutes. (It will finish cooking in the following process.) Leave the oven on.

Meanwhile, thaw and drain the broccoli florets.

Remove the chicken from the baking dish, cool in the refrigerator for 15 minutes, and then cut it into 1-inch (2.5-cm) pieces. Place the chicken back into the baking dish. Add the broccoli.

In an 8- or 9-inch (20- or 22.5-cm) nonstick skillet, melt the light butter over medium-high. Sauté the mushrooms for about 8 minutes, until soft, then distribute them evenly along with any juices over the chicken and broccoli.

In a small mixing bowl, combine the soup, lemon juice, milk, and onions and stir to mix. Pour the mixture over the chicken, broccoli, and mushrooms and bake for 25 minutes.

In a small bowl, mix together the bread crumbs, cheese, and parsley.

Remove the casserole from the oven and sprinkle the bread crumb mixture over the top.

Return the dish to the oven and bake for 10 minutes more, until the crumb topping is golden brown.

YIELD: Makes 8 (about 1-cup) servings.

NUTRITIONAL ANALYSIS
Each with: **Calories:** 161.11 **Protein:** 24.19 g **Carbs:** 8.95 g **Total Fat:** 3.38 g **Sat Fat:** 1.10 g **Cholesterol:** 51.67 mg **Sodium:** 386.20 mg **Sugars:** 2.62 g **Fiber:** 2.16 g

Garlic Shrimp

GBP: Weeks 6–8 Postop

BAND: Weeks 6–8 Postop

BPD: Weeks 6–8 Postop

INGREDIENTS

- 3 pounds (1.5 kg) small shrimp, 21/25 count, shelled and deveined
- ¹/₂ teaspoon sea salt
- ¹/₂ teaspoon fresh cracked pepper
- 2 cloves fresh garlic, minced
- 2 tablespoons (8 g) chopped fresh parsley
- ¹/₂ teaspoon chopped fresh thyme
- ¹/₂ teaspoon chopped fresh oregano
- ¹/₂ teaspoon crushed red chili flakes (optional)
- 3 tablespoons (45 ml) extra-virgin olive oil
- 2 teaspoons fresh lemon juice
- 2 tablespoons (28 ml) cooking sherry
- Lemon wedges
- Fresh whole sprigs parsley

Sprinkle the shrimp with the salt and pepper and let stand for 10 minutes at room temperature.

In a medium bowl, toss the shrimp with the garlic, chopped parsley, thyme, oregano, and red chili flakes (if using).

In an 8-inch (20-cm) skillet, heat the oil over medium to medium-high heat. Cook the shrimp about 3 minutes on each side, until an opaque orange color appears, then add the lemon juice and sherry. Continue cooking for about 2 minutes. Transfer the shrimp to a serving platter along with all of the liquid in the pan. Garnish the dish with the lemon and parsley sprigs for an elegant presentation. Serve immediately.

YIELD: Makes 12 (about 3¹/₂-ounce) servings.

NUTRITIONAL ANALYSIS

Each with: **Calories:** 156.09 **Protein:** 23.11 g **Carbs:** 1.44 g **Total Fat:** 5.48 g **Sat Fat:** 0.87 g **Cholesterol:** 172.37 mg **Sodium:** 224.77 mg **Sugars:** 0.04 g **Fiber:** 0.10 g

Lemon-Barbecue Meatloaf

This is a great dish for the family, or it can be easy divided and frozen for later.

GBP: Weeks 4–6 Postop

BAND: Weeks 4–6 Postop

BPD: Weeks 4–6 Postop

INGREDIENTS

- 2 pounds (1 kg) 95 percent lean ground beef
- 2 cups (320 g) diced yellow onion (about 1¹/₂ onions)
- 2 tablespoons (28 ml) fresh lemon juice
- 7 tablespoons (105 ml) low-carb barbecue sauce, divided
- 2 tablespoons (30 g) low-sodium tomato paste
- 2 tablespoons (8 g) chopped fresh parsley
- ¹/₄ cup (35 g) finely chopped green or red bell pepper
- 1 large egg
- ¹/₄ cup (25 g) bread crumbs
- 6 ¹/₈ -inch (3 mm) thick lemon slices

Preheat the oven to 375°F (190°C, or gas mark 5). Spray a 8¹/₂- x 13¹/₂-inch (22.5- x 32.5-cm) baking dish with cooking spray.

In a large mixing bowl, place the beef, onion, lemon juice, 4 tablespoons (60 ml) of the barbecue sauce, tomato paste, parsley, pepper, egg, and bread crumbs. Mix until well incorporated.

Form the mixture into a loaf and pat it down to condense the consistency. The loaf should touch the width, or short edges of the pan, but leave a few inches of room on both sides of the length.

Bake uncovered for 30 minutes. Remove the loaf from the oven and coat the top with the additional 3 tablespoons (45 ml) barbecue sauce. Place the lemon slices on top of the loaf and return it to the oven. Continue baking for an additional 20 minutes.

YIELD: Makes 12 (about 3-ounce) servings.

NUTRITIONAL ANALYSIS

Each with: **Calories:** 170.19 **Protein:** 22.31 g **Carbs:** 6.04 g **Total Fat:** 5.79 g **Sat Fat:** 2.43 g **Cholesterol:** 75.21 mg **Sodium:** 160.16 mg **Sugars:** 1.91 g **Fiber:** 0.88 g

Savory Ground Turkey Meat Loaf

This is a simple yet delicious dish.

GBP: Weeks 4–6 Postop

BAND: Weeks 4–6 Postop

BPD: Weeks 4–6 Postop

INGREDIENTS

- 2 tablespoons (28 ml) olive oil
- 1 medium onion, diced
- 1/2 medium red pepper, cored, seeded, and diced
- 6–8 white mushrooms, cleaned and sliced very thin
- 1/4 cup (60 ml) white wine
- 1 pound (455 g) lean ground turkey (see note)
- 2/3 cup (65 g) Italian bread crumbs
- 1 egg, beaten
- 1/4 teaspoon black pepper
- 1/2 teaspoon seasoning salt
- 1 teaspoon garlic powder
- 1 tablespoon (4 g) chopped fresh parsley
- 1 tablespoon (15 g) ketchup, plus 1 tablespoon (15 g) additional for the top (optional)
- 2 teaspoons yellow or brown mustard, plus 1 teaspoon for the top (optional)

Preheat the oven to 350°F (180°C, or gas mark 4). Spray a 7- x 9-inch (17.5- x 22.5-cm) baking dish with cooking spray.

In a nonstick pan, heat the oil over medium-high heat. When the oil is hot, add the onion, red pepper, and mushrooms. Sauté the vegetables for 4 to 6 minutes, until softened. Add the wine to deglaze pan. Let the vegetables and wine simmer for 2 to 3 minutes to allow the alcohol to evaporate. Place the pan in the refrigerator and cool completely.

In a large mixing bowl, place the turkey, bread crumbs, egg, black pepper, salt, garlic powder, parsley, 1 tablespoon of the ketchup, and 2 teaspoons of the mustard, along with the cooled sauté mixture. With clean, jewelry-free hands, mix thoroughly. When all the ingredients are mixed together, form a rectangular loaf in the prepared baking dish. Add an additional 1 tablespoon ketchup (if using) and 1 teaspoon mustard (if using) to the top and spread evenly over the turkey loaf to seal in the juices and form a tasty crust. Bake for 45 minutes.

YIELD: Makes 6 (about 3-ounce) servings.

NUTRITIONAL ANALYSIS

Each with **Calories:** 220.40 **Protein:** 22.30 g **Carbs:** 14.38 g **Total Fat:** 7.38 g **Sat Fat:** 1.45 g **Cholesterol:** 76.80 mg **Sodium:** 373.71 mg **Sugars:** 3.82 g **Fiber:** 1.80 g

NOTE

You can use ground white breast meat, 99 percent fat-free, but it will be a bit drier.

Heather's Tasty Marinara Sauce

This recipe is from the kitchen of Heather, a gastric bypass surgery patient in the Boston area. To add protein and texture to this sauce, add up to 1 pound (455 g) of browned spicy Italian sausage, without the skin.

GBP: Weeks 2–4 Postop

BAND: Weeks 2–4 Postop

BPD: Weeks 2–4 Postop

INGREDIENTS

- 3 tablespoons (45 ml) extra-virgin olive oil
- 6 cloves garlic, minced
- 1 medium onion, diced (about 1¹/₂ cups, or 240 g)
- 4 teaspoons dried basil
- 1 teaspoon crushed red chili flakes (optional)
- 3 cans (14¹/₂ ounces, or 415 g each) peeled, crushed low-salt tomatoes

In a 2¹/₂-quart (2.5-L) saucepan, heat the oil over medium-high heat. Add the garlic, onion, basil, and chili flakes (if using) and sauté 4 to 6 minutes, until the onion begins to sweat. Add the tomatoes with the liquid and bring the sauce to a boil, stirring occasionally. Reduce the heat to a simmer and continue cooking for at least 30 minutes.

YIELD: Makes 14 (about ¹/₂-cup) servings.

NUTRITIONAL ANALYSIS
Each with: **Calories:** 53.16 **Protein:** 1.80 g **Carbs:** 5.37 g **Total Fat:** 3.06 g **Sat Fat:** 0.43 g **Cholesterol:** 0.00 mg **Sodium:** 68.39 mg **Sugars:** 3.00 g **Fiber:** 1.16 g

LYNETTE'S NOTE

This is the kind of sauce that tastes even better the next day. In a proper container it should last in the refrigerator up to 5 days. Be sure to cool it completely in the refrigerator before placing a lid on it. This helps to avoid creating an environment that can host bacterial growth, which can thrive in warm and moist food products.

Kosher Lamb Souvlaki

This is a great dish to bring to a barbecue. Serve it with Yogurt-Cucumber Sauce (next page).

GBP: Weeks 6–8 Postop

BAND: Weeks 6–8 Postop

BPD: Weeks 6–8 Postop

INGREDIENTS

- 2 tablespoons (28 ml) extra-virgin olive oil
- 1 tablespoon (10 g) chopped fresh garlic
- 1 teaspoon dried oregano
- 1 teaspoon dried thyme
- 1 teaspoon dried basil
- 2 teaspoons chopped fresh parsley
- $^3/_4$ teaspoon freshly ground black pepper
- $^3/_4$ teaspoon kosher salt
- 1 pound (455 g) lamb, cut from the leg into 12 equal-sized cubes
- 2 yellow bell peppers, cored and cut into 1-inch (2.5-cm) strips
- 1 sweet red onion, cut into 8 large pieces
- 16 cherry tomatoes
- 8 (4-inch, or 10-cm) whole-wheat pitas

Begin preparing a minimum of 3 hours ahead of service time to allow the souvlaki to marinate. (The skewers can marinate for up to 24 hours.)

In a small mixing bowl, mix together the oil, garlic, oregano, thyme, basil, parsley, pepper, and salt, then set aside.

Distribute the lamb, bell peppers, onion, and tomatoes equally onto 8 skewers. Place the skewers in a large shallow pan and evenly pour the marinade over the skewers. Cover the pan and refrigerate at least 3 hours, rotating the skewers once.

Before lighting the grill, spray the rack with cooking spray. Prepare the barbecue grill for medium heat. (If using a charcoal grill, allow the coals to turn a light-ash color.) Place the skewers on the grill and cook 8 to 12 minutes, until the lamb is medium-rare and lightly charred, rotating to cook evenly. Remove the skewers from the grill and let set for 5 minutes. Place one skewer in each pita. Serve immediately.

YIELD: Makes 8 (about 2-ounce) servings.

NUTRITIONAL ANALYSIS
Each with: **Calories:** 225.43 **Protein:** 14.26 g **Carbs:** 21.51 g **Total Fat:** 9.74 g **Sat Fat:** 3.76 g **Cholesterol:** 38.56 mg **Sodium:** 274.53 mg **Sugars:** 3.10 g **Fiber:** 3.28 g

Greek Yogurt-Cucumber Sauce

GBP: Weeks 2-4 Postop

BAND: Weeks 2-4 Postop

BPD: Weeks 2-4 Postop

INGREDIENTS

- 1 cup (135 g) grated cucumber (Squeeze out excess moisture using paper towels.)
- $1/2$ cup (100 g) nonfat sour cream
- 1 container (7 ounces, or 200 g) 2% Greek yogurt
- 1 clove fresh garlic, minced
- 1 teaspoon lemon juice
- $1/4$ teaspoon salt
- $1/8$ teaspoon ground white pepper
- 1 tablespoon (4 g) chopped fresh parsley

In a medium mixing bowl, stir together the cucumber, sour cream, yogurt, garlic, lemon juice, salt, pepper, and parsley with a wire whip. Serve chilled.

YIELD: Makes 10 (about 1-ounce) servings.

NUTRITIONAL ANALYSIS
Each with: **Calories:** 29.40 **Protein:** 2.61 g **Carbs:** 3.68 g **Total Fat:** 0.43 g **Sat Fat:** 0.30 g **Cholesterol:** 3.00 mg **Sodium:** 45.79 mg **Sugars:** 1.80 g **Fiber:** 0.12 g

Mexican Turkey Skillet Casserole

This is a great dish for the whole family.

GBP: Weeks 6-8 Postop

BAND: Weeks 6-8 Postop

BPD: Weeks 6-8 Postop

INGREDIENTS

- ¹/₂ cup (50 g) whole-wheat elbow macaroni
- 1 teaspoon extra-virgin olive oil
- 1 pound (455 g) extra lean ground turkey, 97% fat-free
- 1 teaspoon salt
- 1 tablespoon (9 g) chili powder
- 2 teaspoons paprika
- 2 teaspoons ground cumin
- 2 teaspoons garlic powder
- ¹/₂ teaspoon cayenne pepper (optional)
- 1¹/₂ cups (240 g) diced yellow onion
- 1 can (14¹/₂ ounces, or 415 g) diced tomatoes in juice (no salt added)
- 1 cup (200 g) canned corn (no salt added)
- 4 (8-inch, or 20-cm) low-carb, whole-wheat tortillas
- ¹/₄ cup (50 g) nonfat sour cream
- Fresh sprigs parsley

Preheat the oven to 300°F (150°C, or gas mark 2).

Cook the pasta according to package directions, omitting salt and fat.

While the pasta cooks, heat an 8-inch (20-cm) skillet that has been coated with cooking spray and the oil over medium-high heat. Add the turkey, stirring with a large spoon or rubber spatula. Continue cooking about 15 minutes, stirring just enough to break the turkey into crumbles, and until the turkey begins to brown. Add the salt, chili powder, paprika, cumin, garlic powder, and cayenne pepper (if using), and then stir well to incorporate the spices. Add the onion and continue to cook for 4 to 6 minutes, until the onion begins to soften. Add the tomatoes with the juice and the corn, cover the pan, and continue to cook for 5 minutes.

Wrap the tortillas in aluminum foil and bake for 12 minutes. Remove the tortillas from the foil, roll them into cylinders, and place one on the rim of each dinner plate. On the opposite side of each plate, place 1 tablespoon (12 g) of the sour cream. Spoon one serving in the center of each plate and garnish with a fresh parsley sprig.

YIELD: Makes 4 (1-cup) servings

NUTRITIONAL ANALYSIS

Each with: **Calories:** 319.06 **Protein:** 37.19 g **Carbs:** 35.77 g **Total Fat:** 6.00 g **Sat Fat:** 0.78 g **Cholesterol:** 65.00 mg **Sodium:** 667.49 mg **Sugars:** 10.34 g **Fiber:** 14.31 g

"The Mexican Skillet is just so yummy and spicy. It's similar to a nice chili, a sloppy Joe, or just a good, old-fashioned casserole. It makes you forget that it's good for you."

—Adrienne, *a BPD surgery patient in the Boston area*

MARGARET'S NOTE

This recipe includes 97 percent fat-free ground turkey, but if you can't find this in the market, 93 percent fat-free (no skin) is perfectly acceptable. Enjoy!

One Pot Chicken Dinner in a Pinch

It's fast, easy, and delicious.

GBP: Weeks 6–8 Postop

BAND: Weeks 6–8 Postop

BPD: Weeks 6–8 Postop

INGREDIENTS

- 1 tablespoon (14 ml) olive oil
- 2 teaspoons butter alternative
- 4 medium red potatoes, peeled and thinly sliced
- 1 pound (455 g) boneless, skinless chicken breast, cut into bite-size cubes
- 1 cup (70 g) broccoli fresh florets
- 1 cup (150 g) cauliflower fresh florets
- 1 medium onion, diced
- 1 clove fresh garlic, chopped
- 1 can (10 $^3/_4$ ounces, or 290 g) reduced-fat, low-sodium condensed cream of mushroom soup
- $^1/_2$ cup (120 ml) nonfat milk
- 2 whole green onions, chopped
- 2 tablespoons (8 g) chopped fresh parsley
- $^1/_3$ cup (35 g) grated Parmesan cheese

In a 9- or 10-inch (22.5- or 25-cm) skillet, heat the oil and butter alternative over medium-high heat. Add the potatoes and cook for 15 to 20 minutes, until they begin to brown, stirring occasionally. Add the chicken and continue cooking for about 15 minutes, stirring occasionally, allowing the chicken to brown, then reduce the heat to low.

In a microwave-safe bowl, place the broccoli and cauliflower with water to cover the vegetables and microwave on high power for about 5 minutes, until the broccoli and cauliflower are fork tender. Carefully remove the vegetables from the microwave, drain off all liquid, and add them to the chicken and potatoes, along with the onion and garlic. Add the soup, milk, green onions, parsley, and cheese and stir. Cover the skillet and simmer for 12 to 15 minutes, stirring occasionally. Serve in warm bowls for a complete meal.

YIELD: Makes 8 (about 1-cup) servings.

NUTRITIONAL ANALYSIS

Each with: **Calories:** 244.49 **Protein:** 19.54 g **Carbs:** 25.55 g **Total Fat:** 7.46 g **Sat Fat:** 2.33 g **Cholesterol:** 35.93 mg **Sodium:** 160.87 mg **Sugars:** 4.93 g **Fiber:** 3.20 g

Slow-Cooked Sausage and Lentil Stew

Tasty and satisfying, this can be started in the morning and ready at dinnertime.

GBP: Weeks 6–8 Postop

BAND: Weeks 6–8 Postop

BPD: Weeks 6–8 Postop

INGREDIENTS

- 1¹⁄₂ cups (290 g) lentils, soaked in water for 30 minutes
- ¹⁄₂ cup (50 g) chopped celery
- 2 cups (40 g) chopped fresh spinach, washed and drained
- 3 cloves fresh garlic, coarsely chopped
- 1 cup (160 g) chopped yellow onion
- 4 cups (1 L) water
- 2 tablespoons (30 g) low-sodium tomato paste
- ¹⁄₂ teaspoon cayenne pepper (optional)
- 1 bay leaf
- Juice of ¹⁄₂ lemon (about 2 tablespoons, or 28 ml)
- ¹⁄₂ pound (225 g) light, low-sodium precooked smoked turkey sausage or kielbasa, cut into ¹⁄₄-inch (6-mm) pieces, skin removed (see note)

In a 3-quart (3-L) slow cooker, place all ingredients and cook on the high setting for 5 hours or on the low setting for 7 hours. Remove the bay leaf before serving.

YIELD: Makes 6 (about 1-cup) servings.

NUTRITIONAL ANALYSIS

Each with: **Calories:** 261.32 **Protein:** 20.45 g **Carbs:** 33.07 g **Total Fat:** 6.01 g **Sat Fat:** 0.09 g **Cholesterol:** 23.33 mg **Sodium:** 371.91 mg **Sugars:** 4.87 g **Fiber:** 15.98 g

NOTE

Removing the skin is essential for easier digestion. Score the sausage lengthwise and peel the skin away from the sausage. The skin will come right off.

Roasted Veal with Shallots and Fennel

GBP: Weeks 6–8 Postop

BAND: Weeks 6–8 Postop

BPD: Weeks 6–8 Postop

INGREDIENTS

- 1 tablespoon (19 g) coarse kosher salt
- 2 teaspoons dried basil
- 1 teaspoon dried oregano
- 1 tablespoon (3 g) chopped fresh thyme
- 1 tablespoon (4 g) chopped fresh parsley
- ½ teaspoon ground white pepper
- 3 pounds (1.5 kg) boneless veal shoulder roast
- 2 tablespoons (28 ml) olive oil, divided
- 2 cups (320 g) thinly sliced shallots
- 2 large bulbs fresh fennel, trimmed and thinly sliced
- ½ cup (120 ml) cooking sherry, beef broth, or veal broth
- Fresh herb sprigs

Preheat the oven to 375°F (190°C, or gas mark 5).

In a small mixing bowl, combine the salt, basil, oregano, thyme, parsley, and white pepper and set aside.

Rub the veal evenly and thoroughly with 1 tablespoon (14 ml) of the oil. Coat the veal evenly with the spice mixture, and let stand for 20 minutes in the refrigerator.

In a large skillet, heat the remaining 1 tablespoon (14 ml) oil to medium-high heat. Place the veal in the pan and cook about 6 minutes on each side, until browned on both sides. Remove the veal from the skillet (reserving the brown bits in the bottom) and place it in a 3- or 4-quart (3- or 4-L) roasting pan. Add the shallots and fennel to the skillet and return to medium-high heat. Continue to cook about 15 minutes, until the onion and shallots are brown. Add the sherry or broth to the pan and stir with a spatula to release the brown bits into the liquid. Continue to cook for 2 minutes, then remove from heat. Pour the shallot mixture over the veal and cover it. Bake the veal for about 20 minutes, until the internal temperature at the thickest portion is 160°F. (If a meat thermometer is not available, make an incision in the thickest portion of the roast to determine doneness. Pink throughout indicates medium to medium rare. Pink in the center indicates medium to medium well.) Let the veal stand for 10 minutes before serving. Transfer the veal to a serving platter and arrange the shallot mixture over the top. Garnish the serving dish with fresh herb sprigs.

YIELD: Makes 12 (about 3-ounces veal) servings.

NUTRITIONAL ANALYSIS
Each with: **Calories:** 159.59 **Protein:** 17.35 g **Carbs:** 5.72 g **Total Fat:** 6.47 g **Sat Fat:** 2.18 g **Cholesterol:** 69.74 mg **Sodium:** 483.42 mg **Sugars:** 0.73 g **Fiber:** 1.02 g

Southwestern Marinated Chicken Breast

GBP: Weeks 6–8 Postop

BAND: Weeks 6–8 Postop

BPD: Weeks 6–8 Postop

INGREDIENTS

- 2 tablespoons (28 ml) lime juice (about 2 limes)
- 1/4 cup (60 ml) low-sodium soy sauce
- 1 tablespoon (14 ml) extra-virgin olive oil
- 1 teaspoon oregano
- 1/2 teaspoon paprika
- 1 1/2 teaspoons chili powder
- 1 1/2 teaspoons cumin seed
- 2 tablespoons (15 g) chopped fresh green onion (white and green parts)
- 3 cloves garlic, minced
- 1 1/2 teaspoons honey
- 1/4 cup (60 ml) white wine or lemon juice (optional)
- 2 8-ounce (225 g) whole, boneless, skinless chicken breasts, each cut in half down the middle
- 3 tablespoons (3 g) chopped cilantro leaves
- 1 lime, sliced into 4 slices
- 1/4 cup (70 g) Fresh Salsa Caliente (page 130) (optional)

In a medium mixing bowl, mix together the lime juice, soy sauce, oil, oregano, paprika, chili powder, cumin, green onion, garlic, honey, and wine or lemon juice. Place the chicken in the bowl and cover all surface area with the marinade. Cover the bowl and place it in the refrigerator for at least 1 hour.

Preheat the oven to 375°F (190°C, or gas mark 5). Coat a 7- x 7-inch (17.5- x 17.5-cm) baking dish with cooking spray.

Spray a medium skillet with cooking spray and heat it over medium-high heat. Place the chicken in the pan, smooth side down and brown one side only.

Place the chicken in the prepared baking dish, browned side up, cover it tightly with aluminum foil, and bake for 15 minutes, until chicken is done at the thickest portion. Transfer the chicken to a platter and slice it on a 45-degree angle. Garnish each serving with the cilantro, lime, and salsa (if using).

YIELD: 4 (about 3-ounce) servings.

NUTRITIONAL ANALYSIS

Each with: **Calories:** 196.09 **Protein:** 27.50 g **Carbs:** 5.87 g **Total Fat:** 5.31 g **Sat Fat:** 0.92 g **Cholesterol:** 65.77 mg **Sodium:** 424.03 mg **Sugars:** 3.47 g **Fiber:** 1.04 g

"This marinade was very easy to make. The dish is not too spicy, but it can be adjusted according to your taste by adding extra chili powder and garlic. I love the mixture of the fresh herbs with the wine and lime juice. This great recipe sure is a keeper!"

—Juli, *a gastric bypass surgery patient in the New Bedford, Massachusetts, area*

Spanish Shrimp with Jasmine Rice and Green Beans

GBP: Weeks 6–8 Postop

BAND: Weeks 6–8 Postop

BPD: Weeks 6–8 Postop

INGREDIENTS

- $^3/_4$ cup (135 g) dry jasmine rice
- $1^1/_2$ cups (355 ml) cold water
- 1 pound (455 g) fresh green beans
- 2 cups (475 ml) water
- 1 pound (455 g) medium to large fresh shrimp, peeled and deveined
- $^1/_2$ teaspoon salt
- $^1/_4$ teaspoon black pepper
- 1 tablespoon (14 ml) extra-virgin olive oil
- 1 cup (160 g) julienned sweet onion (cut into $^1/_4$-inch (6-mm) strips
- 2 cloves fresh garlic, minced
- $1^1/_2$ cups (290 g) quartered plum tomatoes, skins removed
- $^1/_2$ cup (120 ml) sherry or chicken broth or vegetable broth
- 2 teaspoons dried oregano
- 1 teaspoon smoked Spanish paprika
- $^1/_8$ teaspoon cayenne pepper (optional)
- $^1/_4$ cup (15 g) chopped fresh parsley
- 5 lemon wedges

Rinse and drain the rice in cold water, then place it in a 1-quart (1-L) saucepan with the $1^1/_2$ cups (355 ml) cold water. Bring the rice to a boil and then reduce the heat to a simmer. Continue to cook, loosely covered, for 20 minutes, until the water is absorbed by the rice.

Wash and drain the green beans. Snap off the stems and any remaining strings. In a $2^1/_2$-quart (2.5-L) saucepan with a steamer basket, place the beans along with the 2 cups (475 ml) water. Cover and bring the water to a boil. Continue to steam the green beans for about 5 minutes, until the desired doneness is reached.

Butterfly the prawns by using a paring knife to score the backside of each one at a depth of about $^1/_4$ inch (6 mm). Place prawns on a plate or sheet pan in a single layer. Sprinkle the salt and pepper on the prawns and set aside.

In an 8-inch (20-cm) skillet, heat the oil over medium-high heat. When the oil is hot, add the onion and garlic and sauté for about 3 minutes, until the onion begins to soften. Add the tomatoes, sherry or broth, oregano, paprika, and cayenne pepper (if using). Reduce the heat to medium-low and continue cooking for 2 minutes. Add the prawns and cook about 5 minutes, until an orange color can be seen throughout each prawn. Remove from the heat.

Divide the rice among five dinner plates. Arrange the prawns around the rice so that the tails are facing upward. Sprinkle each plate with parsley. Arrange the steamed green beans asymmetrically around the prawns. Garnish each plate with a lemon wedge.

YIELD: Makes 5 (about 1-cup) servings.

NUTRITIONAL ANALYSIS

Each with: **Calories:** 296.73 **Protein:** 22.26 g **Carbs:** 34.67 g **Total Fat:** 4.76 g **Sat Fat:** 0.74 g **Cholesterol:** 137.89 mg **Sodium:** 654.61 mg **Sugars:** 5.89 g **Fiber:** 3.67 g

Chicken Curry with Fresh Mint and Shiitake Mushrooms

This dish has a world of complementary flavors!

GBP: Weeks 6–8 Postop

BAND: Weeks 6–8 Postop

BPD: Weeks 6–8 Postop

INGREDIENTS

- ¼ cup (30 g) curry powder
- ½ teaspoon cayenne pepper (optional)
- 1 cup (235 ml) low-sodium chicken broth, divided
- 1 tablespoon (14 ml) extra-virgin olive oil
- 3 chicken breasts, skinless, boneless, trimmed of excess fat, and cut into bite-size pieces (about 3/4-inch, or 19 mm cubes) (see note)
- 1 medium onion, cut into julienne strips (about ¼-inch, or 6-mm thick)
- 5 shiitake mushroom caps, cut into ⅛-inch (3 mm) strips
- ¼ cup white wine or chicken broth or vegetable broth
- 2 cloves fresh garlic, chopped
- 1 tablespoon (8 g) fresh grated gingerroot, peeled
- ½ cup (120 g) plain nonfat yogurt
- 2 tablespoons (2 g) fresh coarsely chopped cilantro, plus additional leaves for garnish
- 1 tablespoon (5 g) chopped fresh mint leaves

In a small bowl, mix the curry powder and cayenne pepper (if using) together with 2 teaspoons of the chicken broth to make a paste and set aside.

Spray a 9-inch (22.5-cm) skillet with cooking spray and heat the oil over medium-high heat.

Add the chicken and sauté 12 to 15 minutes, until it begins to brown. Add the onion and mushrooms and continue to cook 4 to 6 minutes, until the onion begins to soften. Add the curry paste and ¼ cup wine or broth and stir until the chicken is evenly covered. Add a little of the remaining chicken broth at a time, until the desired thickness of the curry sauce is reached. Add the garlic and ginger, stir, and reduce heat to a simmer. Cover the skillet and continue simmering for about 5 minutes, until chicken is done. Slowly add the yogurt and stir in to incorporate. Add the cilantro and mint, stirring to mix well, and return the curry to a simmer. Simmer for an additional 2 minutes and then remove from the heat. Garnish with the cilantro leaves.

YIELD: Makes 6 (about 3½-ounce) servings.

NUTRITIONAL ANALYSIS

Each with: **Calories:** 180.83 **Protein:** 29.52 g **Carbs:** 8.83 g **Total Fat:** 2.00 g **Sat Fat:** 0.48 g **Cholesterol:** 68.86 mg **Sodium:** 421.43 mg **Sugars:** 3.17 g **Fiber:** 1.89 g

NOTE

Fresh shrimp, fresh vegetables, or cubed tofu may be substituted for the chicken.

Baked Chicken Portuguese Style

Creamy Polenta with Fresh Oregano and Feta Cheese (page 148) makes a perfect accompaniment to this extraordinarily tasty chicken dish.

GBP: Weeks 6–8 Postop

BAND: Weeks 6–8 Postop

BPD: Weeks 6–8 Postop

INGREDIENTS

- 1¹/₂ pounds (700 g) boneless, skinless chicken breast, cut into 6 (4-ounce, or 115 g) portions
- ¹/₄ teaspoon salt
- ¹/₄ teaspoon black pepper
- 4 tomatoes, skinned and cut into quarters
- 1 cup (160 g) sliced yellow onion
- 1 cup (140 g) sliced red bell pepper
- ¹/₂ cup (70 g) large pitted black olives or pitted Kalamata olives
- 4 cloves fresh garlic, coarsely chopped
- 1 cup (235 ml) red wine for cooking
- 1¹/₂ cups (355 ml) water
- ¹/₄ cup (60 ml) fresh lemon juice (about 1 lemon)

Preheat the oven to 375°F (190°C, or gas mark 5).

Season the chicken with the salt and pepper and let stand for 10 to 15 minutes at room temperature.

Spray a 10-inch (25-cm) skillet with cooking spray and heat it over medium-high heat. Place the chicken in the hot pan and brown one side only. Transfer the chicken to a 7¹/₂- x 11¹/₂ -inch (17.5- x 27.5-cm) baking dish, with the browned sides facing up.

Add the tomatoes, onions, bell pepper, olives, garlic, red wine, water, and lemon juice so the ingredients are evenly dispersed over the chicken. Bake for approximately 20 minutes, until the chicken is cooked throughout. (Make a small incision in the thickest portion of the chicken. The juice should run clear.)

YIELD: Makes 6 (about 3-ounce) servings.

NUTRITIONAL ANALYSIS

Each with: **Calories:** 314.39 **Protein:** 31.16 g **Carbs:** 34.55 g **Total Fat:** 6.01 g **Sat Fat:** 0.70 g **Cholesterol:** 65.77 mg **Sodium:** 339.83 mg **Sugars:** 19.66 g **Fiber:** 8.93 g

Eggplant Parmesan

GBP: Weeks 6–8 Postop

BAND: Weeks 6–8 Postop

BPD: Weeks 6–8 Postop

INGREDIENTS

- 1 large eggplant (about 1¹/₄ pounds, or 570 g)
- ¹/₂ teaspoon salt
- 1 tablespoon (14 ml) olive oil
- ¹/₂ cup (80 g) diced yellow onion
- 2 cans (11 ounces, or 310 g each) tomato sauce, no salt added
- 1 teaspoon dried basil
- 1 teaspoon dried oregano
- ¹/₄ cup (15 g) chopped fresh parsley
- 1 teaspoon dried thyme
- 1 cup (110 g) part skim-milk mozzarella cheese
- 1 tablespoon (5 g) grated Parmesan cheese

Preheat the oven to 375°F (190°C, or gas mark 5). Spray a 9- x 13-inch (22.5- x 32.5-cm) baking dish with cooking spray.

Remove the skin and stem from the eggplant with a vegetable peeler or a small kitchen knife.

Cut the eggplant into ¼-inch (6-mm) circles and arrange them overlapping in the prepared baking dish. Evenly sprinkle the eggplant slices with the salt. Drizzle the oil on top of the eggplant. Distribute the onions evenly on top of the eggplant. Pour the tomato sauce evenly on top of the eggplant, allowing it to disperse throughout the slices. Evenly sprinkle the basil, oregano, parsley, and thyme on top of the sauce. Spread the mozzarella and Parmesan over the top. Bake for 30 to 40 minutes, until the cheese is bubbly and golden brown.

YIELD: Makes 6 (about 1-cup) servings.

NUTRITIONAL ANALYSIS

Each with: **Calories:** 138.58 **Protein:** 6.85 g **Carbs:** 14.72 g **Total Fat:** 6.01 g **Sat Fat:** 2.55 g **Cholesterol:** 10.73 mg **Sodium:** 233.87 mg **Sugars:** 7.16 g **Fiber:** 5.03 g

Spaghetti Squash with Pomodoro Sauce

This is a wonderful substitute for pasta in a delicious sauce.

GBP: Weeks 6–8 Postop

BAND: Weeks 6–8 Postop

BPD: Weeks 6–8 Postop

INGREDIENTS

- 1 medium spaghetti squash (enough to yield 2 cups, or 310 g cooked)
- 1½ cups (570 ml) water
- 1 can (14 1/5 ounces, or 415 g) diced tomatoes in juice, no salt added
- 2 cloves garlic, minced
- 6 tablespoons (3 ounces, or 90 ml) white wine or chicken broth or vegetable broth
- ½ teaspoon kosher salt
- ½ teaspoon ground white pepper
- 1 tablespoon (14 ml) extra-virgin olive oil
- 1 tablespoon (5 g) grated Parmesan cheese
- Fresh parsley sprigs

Preheat the oven to 375° (190°C, or gas mark 5).

Cut the squash in half lengthwise and scrape out and discard the seeds. Place the halves in a baking dish, skin sides up. Add the water to the baking dish and bake about 40 minutes, until the squash will gently peel away from the skin with a fork.

In a 1- or 2-quart (1- or 2-L) saucepan, place the tomatoes with juice, garlic, wine or broth, salt, white pepper, and oil, cover, and bring to a simmer. Once a simmer is reached, remove the cover and continue cooking for 20 minutes.

For a smoother consistency, an emersion blender can be used to slightly puree the sauce.

Remove the cooked spaghetti squash by gently peeling away from the skin with a fork. Arrange in 1-cup (155 g) mounds on serving plates or in serving bowls as you would pasta and top with the sauce. Garnish with the cheese and parsley.

YIELD: Makes 4 (about ³/₄-cup) servings.

NUTRITIONAL ANALYSIS

Each with: **Calories:** 96.47 **Protein:** 1.80 g **Carbs:** 10.21 g **Total Fat:** 4.01 g **Sat Fat:** 0.69 g **Cholesterol:** 0.25 mg **Sodium:** 274.69 mg **Sugars:** 4.29 g **Fiber:** 2.09 g

MARGARET'S NOTE

This delicious dish provides almost half of your vitamin C for the day. If you'd like to make a complete meal out of this, add about 3 ounces (85 g) shredded part-skim mozzarella cheese or shredded vegetarian (soy) cheese.

MARGARET'S NOTE

*You could add ¾ cup of soy or vegetarian cheese to this
recipe. Add it while making the potato topping or grate it
on top of the finished dish. Also, you could substitute
adzuki beans or green or yellow split peas instead of all, or
some, of the lentils.*

Vegetarian Shepherd's Pie

Lentils make this dish high in fiber, hearty, and delicious.

GBP: Weeks 6–8 Postop

BAND: Weeks 6–8 Postop

BPD: Weeks 6–8 Postop

INGREDIENTS

- 1$\frac{1}{2}$ cups (290 g) green or brown lentils
- 1$\frac{1}{2}$ pounds (700 g) russet potatoes
- 3 tablespoons (45 g) light butter, divided
- 1 small yellow onion, diced (about $\frac{3}{4}$ cup, or 120 g)
- $\frac{1}{2}$ cup (65 g) chopped carrot (about 1 medium)
- 1 medium celery rib, halved lengthwise and thinly sliced
- 2 cloves garlic, chopped
- 1 teaspoon salt
- $\frac{1}{2}$ teaspoon black pepper
- 1 teaspoon dried basil
- 1 teaspoon dried oregano
- 1 teaspoon dried thyme
- $\frac{1}{4}$ teaspoon cayenne pepper (optional)
- $\frac{1}{4}$ cup (15 g) chopped fresh parsley
- 2 medium tomatoes, cored and diced
- 2 tablespoons (28 ml) soy milk, unsweetened
- $\frac{3}{4}$ cup (85 g) soy Cheddar cheese (optional)
- $\frac{1}{2}$ teaspoon paprika

In a bowl with water, soak the lentils for 30 minutes.

Peel and dice the potatoes into about 1-inch (2.5-cm) cubes. Place the potatoes in a 2$\frac{1}{2}$ -quart (2.5-L) saucepan with cold water to cover about 1 inch (2.5 cm) above the level of the potatoes.

Bring the potatoes to a boil and continue cooking for about 12 minutes, until the potatoes are tender throughout and will mash easily with a fork. Drain the potatoes in a colander and set aside.

In a 2-quart (2-L) saucepan, place the lentils with 3 cups (705 ml) of cold water and bring them to a boil. Reduce the heat to a simmer, loosely cover the pot, and continue cooking for about 30 minutes, or until all the liquid is absorbed and the lentils are tender.

Preheat the oven to 350°F (180°C, or gas mark 4). Coat a 2-quart (2-L) deep baking dish with cooking spray.

In a 9- or 10-inch (22.5- or 25-cm) skillet, melt 1 tablespoon (14 g) of the butter alternative over medium-high heat. Add the onion, carrots, celery, garlic, salt, pepper, basil, oregano, thyme, and cayenne pepper (if using) and sauté for about 5 minutes, until the carrots begin to soften, stirring occasionally. Add the parsley and tomatoes and continue to cook for about 3 minutes. Remove from the heat.

Mash the cooked lentils slightly with a large serving spoon and add them to the vegetable mixture, stirring just enough to incorporate. Spread the mixture evenly in the prepared baking dish and set aside.

Mash the potatoes together with 2 tablespoons (28 g) of the butter alternative, the soy milk, and soy cheese. Distribute the mashed potatoes over the lentil-vegetable mixture and bake in the oven for 30 minutes, until the top appears golden brown. Serve hot and garnish with the paprika.

YIELD: Makes 8 (about 1-cup) servings.

NUTRITIONAL ANALYSIS

Each with: **Calories:** 235.36 **Protein:** 13.11 g **Carbs:** 41.55 g **Total Fat:** 3.06 g **Sat Fat:** 0.49 g **Cholesterol:** 0.00 mg **Sodium:** 214.17 mg **Sugars:** 5.04 g **Fiber:** 14.63 g

Tasty Baked Tofu
with Sautéed Spinach

Delicious vegetarian meals don't come easier than this.

GBP: Weeks 6–8 Postop

BAND: Weeks 6–8 Postop

BPD: Weeks 6–8 Postop

INGREDIENTS

- 2 tablespoons (28 ml) light soy sauce
- ⅛ teaspoon toasted sesame oil
- 2 tablespoons (28 ml) apple cider vinegar
- 1 clove garlic, minced
- 1 package (16 ounces, 455 g) firm tofu, drained and cut into cubes or cutlets
- 10 cups (200 g) fresh spinach
- 2 teaspoons extra-virgin olive oil
- 1 clove garlic, sliced into thin strips
- Juice of 1 lemon
- ½ teaspoon black pepper

In a 7- or 8-inch (17.5- or 20-cm) baking dish, place the soy sauce, sesame oil, vinegar, and minced garlic. Add the tofu. Marinate for 1 hour, turning the tofu once to expose all sides to the marinade.

Preheat the oven to 350°F (180°C, or gas mark 4).

Drain the excess marinade from the tofu and discard. Bake the tofu for approximately 30 minutes.

Meanwhile, wash, drain, and chop the spinach into 1-inch (2.5-cm) strips. (If using baby spinach, leave it in whole leaves.) Pat the spinach dry with a paper towel.

In an 8-inch (20-cm) skillet, heat the oil over medium heat. Add the sliced garlic and sauté just enough to sweat the garlic. (Do not brown.) Add the spinach, lemon juice, and pepper. Cook for about 4 to 6 minutes, stirring often, until the spinach is tender. Place the spinach on a serving dish and top with the tofu.

YIELD: Makes 4 (about ½-cup) servings.

NUTRITIONAL ANALYSIS
Each with: **Calories:** 224.85 **Protein:** 23.89 g **Carbs:** 19.95 g **Total Fat:** 5.83 g **Sat Fat:** 0.33 g **Cholesterol:** 0.00 mg **Sodium:** 1492.84 mg **Sugars:** 1.56 g **Fiber:** 10.09 g

MARGARET'S NOTE

This dish is a bit higher in sodium than normally recommended (usually 700 milligrams or less per meal, for those who are salt-sensitive and/or need to watch sodium intake for blood pressure reasons), but it may be suitable for most people. If sodium is not an issue, you may add a bit of kosher salt to the spinach for added flavor. Also, you can increase the protein content of this dish by adding shredded soy cheese to the spinach. Another option is to toast about $^1/_8$ to $^1/_4$ cup (12 to 25 g) of slivered almonds and sprinkle on top. This will add a bit more fat, but no cholesterol, and it will also increase the protein content.

CHAPTER 10

Desserts

Lemon Sorbet

Lemon sorbet is a tasty and refreshing finish to any meal, from a casual barbecue, to your finest dinner.

GBP: Weeks 2–4 Postop

BAND: Weeks 2–4 Postop

BPD: Weeks 2–4 Postop

INGREDIENTS

- 5 large lemons
- 2 limes
- 1³/₄ cups (50 g) sugar substitute, suitable for baking (see page 38)
- 1 tablespoon (5 g) chopped fresh mint leaves
- Sprigs fresh mint

Cut the tops off of 4 of the lemons, about one-fourth of the way down from the top.

With a spoon, scoop out the insides over a bowl to catch the juice and pulp. Reserve the whole lemon peel cups. Zest or grate the lemon peel tops and set the zest aside. Discard the tops. Squeeze all the lemon juice from the pulp and discard the pulp. Cut the remaining lemon in half, juice it and combine it with the rest of the juice. Zest or grate the outside peel of the fifth lemon, and add it to the juice, along with the zest from the four tops.

Juice the limes and add this to the lemon juice. Add the sugar substitute and mint leaves. Place all the combined juice in a 4-cup (940 ml) measuring container and add water to make 4 cups (940 ml) total liquid. Pour the mixture into ice cube trays and freeze the mixture overnight. Remove from the freezer and place in a food processor fitted with a metal S blade or a blender and blend until smooth. Return the mixture to the freezer until it is firm, but still soft enough to scoop, for 45 minutes to 1 hour. Scoop the sorbet into the reserved lemon cups and freeze until ready to serve. Garnish with the mint sprigs.

YIELD: Makes 4 (6-ounce) servings.

NUTRITIONAL ANALYSIS

Each with: **Calories:** 37.05 **Protein:** 1.85 g **Carbs:** 17.98 g **Total Fat:** 0.47 g **Sat Fat:** 0.06 g **Cholesterol:** 0.00 mg **Sodium:** 4.72 mg **Sugars:** 2.89 g **Fiber:** 7.28 g

Sugar-Free Ginger Applesauce Cake

This is acceptable for diabetic needs, yet oh-so-tasty!

GBP: Weeks 6–8 Postop

BAND: Weeks 6–8 Postop

BPD: Weeks 6–8 Postop

INGREDIENTS

- 2 cups (220 g) all-purpose flour
- 1 teaspoon baking powder
- 1 teaspoon baking soda
- 1¹/₂ teaspoons allspice
- ¹/₂ teaspoon salt
- ³/₄ cup (20 g) brown sugar substitute
- 2 eggs
- 2 tablespoons (16 g) fresh grated gingerroot
- 1¹/₂ cups (360 g) unsweetened applesauce
- 1¹/₂ teaspoons vanilla extract

Preheat the oven to 350°F (180°C, or gas mark 4). Spray a 1¹/₂-quart (1.5-L) loaf pan with cooking spray.

In a medium mixing bowl, sift together the flour, baking powder, baking soda, allspice, and salt.

In a separate bowl, mix together the sugar substitute, eggs, ginger, applesauce, and vanilla.

Pour the wet mixture into the dry mixture in thirds, stirring all the while with a wire whisk. Continue mixing until just smooth. (Do not over mix.) Pour the batter into the prepared pan and bake for about 50 minutes, until a toothpick inserted into the center comes out clean. Cool the cake at room temperature for 30 minutes before releasing it from the pan.

YIELD: Makes 12 (about 2-ounce) servings.

NUTRITIONAL ANALYSIS

Each with: **Calories:** 106.71 **Protein:** 3.35 g **Carbs:** 20.23 g **Total Fat:** 1.07 g **Sat Fat:** 0.29 g **Cholesterol:** 40.00 mg **Sodium:** 198.57 mg **Sugars:** 3.64 g **Fiber:** 0.84 g

Holiday Pumpkin Parfait

This is a fast, beautiful, low-fat, and delicious dessert for a holiday or any occasion.

GBP: Weeks 2–4 Postop

BAND: Weeks 2–4 Postop

BPD: Weeks 2–4 Postop

INGREDIENTS

- 1 cup (255 g) pumpkin puree
- 1 package (1 ounce, 28 g) sugar-free instant vanilla pudding mix
- 2 cups (475 ml) cold nonfat milk
- 1 teaspoon cinnamon
- 1 teaspoon allspice
- 1/2 teaspoon vanilla extract
- 6 tablespoons (18 g) nonfat whipped cream topping
- 6 cinnamon sticks
- 1/2 teaspoon ground nutmeg

In a medium mixing bowl, combine the pumpkin puree, pudding mix, and milk. Add the cinnamon, allspice, and vanilla and mix thoroughly. Evenly spoon the mixture into 6 parfait or martini glasses. Chill in the refrigerator for about 30 minutes, until the mixture sets. Place 1 tablespoon (3 g) whipped cream topping on top of each parfait. Garnish each one with a cinnamon stick and the nutmeg.

YIELD: Makes 6 (about 1/2-cup) servings.

NUTRITIONAL ANALYSIS

Each with: **Calories:** 55.44 g **Protein:** 3.28 g **Carbs:** 9.43 g **Total Fat:** 0.87 g **Sat Fat:** 0.46 g **Cholesterol:** 1.63 mg **Sodium:** 99.91 mg **Sugars:** 5.41 g **Fiber:** 1.50 g

Baked Pears with Vanilla Ice Cream

This is a scrumptious and elegant dessert for your finest dinner party.

GBP: Weeks 6–8 Postop

BAND: Weeks 6–8 Postop

BPD: Weeks 6–8 Postop

INGREDIENTS

- 1 teaspoon light butter, melted
- 2 teaspoons cream sherry or 1 teaspoon lemon juice mixed with 1 teaspoon sugar-free vanilla syrup
- 1 tablespoon (14 ml) sugar-free maple syrup
- 4 Anjou pears
- 2 cups (270 g) sugar-free, light vanilla ice cream
- 8 cinnamon sticks

Preheat the oven to 375°F (190°C, or gas mark 5).

In a medium mixing bowl, combine the melted butter, cream sherry or lemon juice and syrup, and maple syrup.

Skin, cut in half lengthwise, and core the pears. (Use a spoon to remove the core of the pear, forming a cup in the center.) Place the pears in the bowl with the marinade and gently toss to cover all surface area of the pears. Marinate the pears for about 30 minutes, gently turning them in the marinade three or four times. Place the pears cut sides down in a baking dish large enough to hold the pears and pour the marinade over the top. Bake the pears for about 30 minutes, until caramel begins to form on the outside. Remove the pears from the oven, let cool slightly, and place on dessert dishes, cut sides up. Fill each pear center with a scoop of the ice cream, garnish with a cinnamon stick, and serve warm.

YIELD: Makes 8 (1/2-pear and 1/4-cup ice cream) servings

NUTRITIONAL ANALYSIS
Each with: **Calories:** 104.31 **Protein:** 1.67 g **Carbs:** 20.16 g **Total Fat:** 2.88 g **Sat Fat:** 1.42 g **Cholesterol:** 9.18 mg **Sodium:** 37.29 mg **Sugars:** 10.37 g **Fiber:** 2.81 g

Fat-Free Ricotta with Raspberries and Honey

This simple and elegant dessert is worthy of your finest dinner parties, and it's almost fat-free. It's a small, but super rich and satisfying dessert.

GBP: Weeks 4–6 Postop

BAND: Weeks 4–6 Postop

BPD: Weeks 3–6 Postop

INGREDIENTS

- 1 pound (455 g) nonfat ricotta cheese
- 1 cup (125 g) fresh raspberries
- 1 teaspoon sweetened vanilla powder
- 1 tablespoon (14 ml) honey
- 4 sprigs fresh mint
- 8 low-calorie, low-carb gourmet cookies

Divide the cheese among four small custard cups or dessert dishes. Place the raspberries over the top and around the cheese. Using a small sieve, sprinkle the vanilla powder equally over the top of each. Drizzle the honey evenly over each top. Garnish each dessert with a fresh mint sprig and 2 cookies. Use the cookies for spoons.

YIELD: Makes 8 (about ¼-cup) servings

NUTRITIONAL ANALYSIS

Each with: **Calories:** 125.50 **Protein:** 9.18 g **Carbs:** 22.84 g **Total Fat:** 1.10 g **Sat Fat:** 0.00 g **Cholesterol:** 6.00 mg **Sodium:** 90.15 mg **Sugars:** 13.68 g **Fiber:** 1.50 g

Index

A

Alcohol guidelines, 11
All-American Scramble, 44
Appetizers and entertaining at home, 130–147
　Curry Yogurt Dip, 131
　Easy and Delicious Spinach Dip, 138
　Fresh Salsa Caliente, 132
　Hot Artichoke Dip, 135
　Latkes, 141
　Pacific Dungeness Crab Cakes, 143
　Plum Tomatoes with Blue Cheese, 144
　Roasted Garlic, 136
　Smoked Salmon Dip, 140
　Stuffed Mushrooms, 145
　Sweet Corn Relish, 130
　Toasted Pita Chips, 136
　Traditional Hummus, 146
　Vegetable Party Platter, 130
Artificial sweeteners, 38–39
　Equal and NutraSweet (aspartame), 38
　information resources, 39
　Splenda, 38
　Stevie (sweet leaf), 38–39
　sugar alcohols (sorbitol, mannitol), 39
　Sunette (acesulfame potassium), 39
　Sweet'N Low and Sugar Twin (saccharin), 38
Asian Chicken Wrap, 86
Asian-Influenced Cabbage Medley, 123
Avocado, Cream Cheese, and Bacon Sandwich, 76
Awesome Egg Salad Sandwich, 82

B

Bacon, Tomato, Lettuce, and Cream Cheese Sandwich, 82
Bacon-Cheddar Muffins, 72
Baked Chicken Portuguese Style, 218
Baked Ham and Cheese Sandwich, 80
Baked Pears with Vanilla Ice Cream, 232
Baked Sea Bass, 186
Bariatric surgery
　blood tests prior to, 14
　statistics, 6
　types, 6
Beans
　Black Bean Soup, 101
　Channa Dal, 156
　Edamame, 161
　Green Bean Casserole, 153
　Lobster and Scallop Sauté with Fresh Steamed Green Beans, 180
　Marinated Vegetable Salad in Creamy Vinaigrette, 120
　Slow-Cooked Bone-In White Chicken Chili, 192
　Spanish Shrimp with Jasmine Rice and Green Beans, 214

Traditional Hummus, 146
Beef
　Ground Beef and Spinach Scramble, 46
　Lemon-Barbecue Meatloaf, 201
　Pot Roast á la Sara, 198
Berry Delicious Cream of Wheat, 55
Berry-Mango Breakfast Shake, 56
Best Ever Tofu Burger, 83
Biliopancreatic diversion (BPD), 8–9, 32–37
　bacterial overgrowth, 36
　carbonated beverages after, 36
　chewing gum and, 36
　decreased appetite, 35
　description of surgery, 32–33
　diet after surgery, 36–37
　lactose intolerance, 36
　mealtime considerations, 33–34
　medications absorption, 34
　protein guidelines and, 11
　protein importance, 34–35
　sugars, avoid concentrated, 35–36
　vitamin and mineral absorption, 33
　wheat gluten and, 36
Black Bean Soup, 101
Blue Cheese Dressing, 126
Boiled New Potatoes with Fresh Parsley, 165
Boneless Chicken Breast Cacciatore, 194
Breaded Grouper Fillets, 181
Breads, notes about, 76
Breakfast Turkey Sausage Patties, 62
Breakfasts and brunches, 44–72
　All-American Scramble, 44
　Bacon-Cheddar Muffins, 72
　Berry Delicious Cream of Wheat, 55
　Berry-Mango Breakfast Shake, 56
　Breakfast Turkey Sausage Patties, 62
　Carrot Muffins with Fresh Dill, 68
　Cheese and Pepper Omelet, 51
　Cumin Mushroom Omelet, 54
　Denver Scramble, 45
　Fresh Herb and Goat Cheese Scramble, 49
　Fresh Strawberry Muffins, 69
　Frozen Fruit Smoothie, 58
　Greek High-Protein Berry-Licious Milkshake, 57
　Greek Scramble, 47
　Green Chili and Cheese Cornbread Muffins, 70
　Ground Beef and Spinach Scramble, 46
　Italian Scramble, 49
　Lavender-Blueberry Muffins, 67
　Mark's Fruity French Toast, 52
　Mushroom and Swiss Cheese Scramble, 47
　Savory Broccoli and Cheese Bread Pudding, 61

Spanish Omelet, 50
Spring Herb and Zucchini Muffins, 66
Tomato and Fresh Basil Scramble, 48
Zucchini, Bacon, and Swiss Cheese Scramble, 48
Zucchini and Potato Strata, 65
Zucchini-Bran Muffins, 71
Zucchini Frittata with Capers and Olives, 63
Broccoli
　Broccoli Raab, 155
　Chicken, Broccoli, and Mushroom Casserole, 195
　Easy Broccoli and Cottage Cheese Casserole, 148
　Mandarin Orange Broccoli, 159
　One Pot Chicken Dinner in a Pinch, 207
　Savory Broccoli and Cheese Bread Pudding, 61
Broccoli Raab, 155
Brussels Hash, 149
Butter substitutes, 43

C

Caffeinated drinks guidelines, 10–11
Cajun Blackened Rub, 171
Carbohydrates guidelines, 12
Carbonated beverages guidelines, 11
Carrot Muffins with Fresh Dill, 68
Channa Dal, 156
Cheese
　Avocado, Cream Cheese, and Bacon Sandwich, 76
　Bacon, Tomato, Lettuce, and Cream Cheese Sandwich, 82
　Bacon-Cheddar Muffins, 72
　Baked Ham and Cheese Sandwich, 80
　Black Bean Soup, 101
　Blue Cheese Dressing, 126
　Cheese and Pepper Omelet, 51
　Classic Turkey, Cranberry, and Cream Cheese Sandwich, 78
　Classic Turkey and Swiss Wrap, 74
　Creamy Italian Dressing, 127
　Creamy Polenta with Fresh Oregano and Feta Cheese, 150
　Cumin Mushroom Omelet, 54
　Cumin Mushroom Quesadillas, 73
　Curry Yogurt Dip, 131
　Dill Dressing, 129
　Easy Broccoli and Cottage Cheese Casserole, 148
　Eggplant Parmesan, 221
　Fat-Free Ricotta with Raspberries and Honey, 233
　French Dressing, 127
　Fresh Herb and Goat Cheese Scramble, 49
　Fresh Mozzarella, Tomato, and

Tapenade Sandwich, 80
Garden Goddess Dressing, 128
Greek Salad, 114
Green Bean Casserole, 153
Green Chili and Cheese Cornbread
  Muffins, 70
Herb and Cheese Mashed Cauliflower,
  162
Horseradish Dressing, 129
Hot Artichoke Dip, 135
Latkes, 141
Mushroom and Swiss Cheese Scramble,
  47
One Pot Chicken Dinner in a Pinch, 207
Pita Pizza, 89
Plum Tomatoes with Blue Cheese, 144
Radicchio and Cauliflower Salad with
  Roasted Walnuts, 116
Savory Broccoli and Cheese Bread
  Pudding, 61
Smoked Salmon Dip, 140
Sweet Lemon Poppy Seed Dressing,
  128
Sweet Potatoes au Gratin, 166
Turkey Sandwich with Cucumbers and
  Herbed Cream Cheese, 81
Vegetarian Shepherd's Pie, 225
Zucchini, Bacon, and Swiss Cheese
  Scramble, 48
Zucchini and Potato Strata, 65
Zucchini Frittata with Capers and
  Olives, 63
Cheese and Pepper Omelet, 51
Chicken
  Asian Chicken Wrap, 86
  Boneless Chicken Breast Cacciatore, 194
  Chicken, Broccoli, and Mushroom
    Casserole, 195
  Chicken Curry with Fresh Mint and
    Shiitake Mushrooms, 217
  Easy Oven-Baked "Fried" Chicken, 212
  Maria and Karen's Zesty Lemon and
    Caper Chicken, 193
  Mediterranean Chicken Salad Sandwich,
    77
  notes about, 177
  One Pot Chicken Dinner in a Pinch, 207
  Pita Pizza, 89
  Portuguese Style Baked Chicken, 218
  Slow-Cooked Bone-In White Chicken
    Chili, 192
  Southwestern Marinated Chicken
    Breast, 211
  Whole Roasted Chicken with Potatoes
    and Brussels Sprouts, 176
  Zesty Broiled Marinated Chicken, 213
Chicken, Broccoli, and Mushroom
  Casserole, 195
Chicken Curry with Fresh Mint and

Shiitake Mushrooms, 217
Chilled Honeydew Soup with Spearmint,
  96
Chive-Yogurt Sauce
Citrus-Roasted Carrots with Honey, 169
Classic Spinach Salad with Apple Cider
  Vinaigrette, 107
Classic Turkey, Cranberry, and Cream
  Cheese Sandwich, 78
Classic Turkey and Swiss Wrap, 74
Colander, 42
Creamy Italian Dressing, 127
Creamy Lemon Herb Dressing, 126
Creamy Polenta with Fresh Oregano and
  Feta Cheese, 150
Creamy Tomato Parmesan Soup, 100
Cumin Mushroom Omelet, 54
Cumin Mushroom Quesadillas, 73
Curried Carrot Soup, 92
Curried Pork Loin Roast with Currants,
  Apples, and Sweet Onions, 178-179
Curry Dry Rub, 173
Curry Yogurt Dip, 131

D
Denver Scramble, 45
Desserts, 228–233
  Baked Pears with Vanilla Ice Cream,
    232
  Fat-Free Ricotta with Raspberries and
    Honey, 233
  Holiday Pumpkin Parfait, 231
  Lemon Sorbet, 229
  Sugar-Free Ginger Applesauce Cake,
    229
Dill Dressing, 129
Dill Rub, 170
Dinners, 175–227
  Baked Sea Bass, 186
  Boneless Chicken Breast Cacciatore,
    194
  Breaded Grouper Fillets, 181
  Chicken, Broccoli, and Mushroom
    Casserole, 195
  Chicken Curry with Fresh Mint and
    Shiitake Mushrooms, 217
  Curried Pork Loin Roast with Currants,
    Apples, and Sweet Onions, 178-179
  Easy Oven-Baked "Fried" Chicken, 212
  Eggplant Parmesan, 221
  Fillet of Salmon á la Herman, 189
  Fillet of Salmon with Sesame-Orange
    Glaze, 185
  Fillet of Sole with Vegetables Baked in
    Parchment, 183
  Fresh Citrus Grilled Shrimp, 184
  Garlic Shrimp, 197
  Grilled Salmon with Toasted Fennel and
    Paprika, 190

Heather's Tasty Marinara Sauce, 203
Kosher Lamb Souvlaki, 204
Lemon-Barbecue Meatloaf, 201
Lobster and Scallop Sauté with Fresh
  Steamed Green Beans, 180
Maria and Karen's Zesty Lemon and
  Caper Chicken, 193
Mexican Turkey Skillet Casserole, 206
One Pot Chicken Dinner in a Pinch, 207
Pork Tenderloin Medallions with Spanish
  Smoked Paprika, 175
Portuguese Style Baked Chicken, 218
Pot Roast á la Sara, 198
Roasted Veal with Shallots and Fennel,
  210
Savory Ground Turkey Meat Loaf, 202
Slow-Cooked Bone-In White Chicken
  Chili, 192
Slow-Cooked Sausage and Lentil Stew,
  208
Southwestern Marinated Chicken
  Breast, 211
Spaghetti Squash with Pomodoro
  Sauce, 222
Spanish Shrimp with Jasmine Rice and
  Green Beans, 214
Tasty Baked Tofu with Sautéed
  Spinach, 226
Vegetarian Shepherd's Pie, 225
Whole Roasted Chicken with Potatoes
  and Brussels Sprouts, 176
Zesty Broiled Marinated Chicken, 213
Dressings for salads. See Salads and
  dressings; Vinaigrettes
Drinks
  Berry-Mango Breakfast Shake, 56
  Frozen Fruit Smoothie, 58
  Greek High-Protein Berry-Licious
    Milkshake, 57
Dry Jamaican Jerk Rub, 171

E
Easy and Delicious Spinach Dip, 138
Easy Broccoli and Cottage Cheese
  Casserole, 148
Easy Oven-Baked "Fried" Chicken, 212
Edamame, 161
Eggplant Parmesan, 221
Eggs
  All-American Scramble, 44
  Awesome Egg Salad Sandwich, 82
  Cheese and Pepper Omelet, 51
  Cumin Mushroom Omelet, 54
  Denver Scramble, 45
  Fresh Herb and Goat Cheese Scramble,
    49
  Greek Scramble, 47
  Ground Beef and Spinach Scramble, 46
  Italian Scramble, 49

Mushroom and Swiss Cheese Scramble,
47
protein powder, 41
Spanish Omelet, 50
Tomato and Fresh Basil Scramble, 48
Zucchini, Bacon, and Swiss Cheese
Scramble, 48
Ethiopian Spice Mix, 174

F
Fall Harvest Pumpkin Soup, 95
Fat-Free Ricotta with Raspberries and
Honey, 233
Fats guidelines, 13
Fearsome Garlic Pork Rub, 174
Fiber guidelines, 12–13
Fillet of Salmon á la Herman, 189
Fillet of Salmon with Sesame-Orange
Glaze, 185
Fillet of Sole with Vegetables Baked in
Parchment, 183
Fish. *See* Seafood
Fluid guidelines, 10–11
Food processor, 42
French Dressing, 127
Fresh Citrus Grilled Shrimp, 184
Fresh Fruit Salad, 121
Fresh Herb and Goat Cheese Scramble,
49
Fresh Mozzarella, Tomato, and Tapenade
Sandwich, 80
Fresh Salsa Caliente, 132
Fresh Strawberry Muffins, 69
Frozen Fruit Smoothie, 58
Fruit
Baked Pears with Vanilla Ice Cream,
232
Berry Delicious Cream of Wheat, 55
Berry-Mango Breakfast Shake, 56
Carrot Muffins with Fresh Dill, 68
Chilled Honeydew Soup with
Spearmint, 96
Curried Pork Loin Roast with Currants,
Apples, and Sweet Onions, 178-179
Fat-Free Ricotta with Raspberries and
Honey, 233
Fillet of Salmon with Sesame-Orange
Glaze, 185
Fresh Fruit Salad, 121
Fresh Strawberry Muffins, 69
Frozen Fruit Smoothie, 58
Greek High-Protein Berry-Licious
Milkshake, 57
Lavender-Blueberry Muffins, 67
Lemon Sorbet, 228
Mandarin Orange Broccoli, 159
Mandarin Pea Pod Salad, 107
Mark's Fruity French Toast, 52
Roasted Beets and Mango Salad, 119
Sugar-Free Ginger Applesauce Cake,
229
Zucchini-Bran Muffins, 71

G
Garden Goddess Dressing, 128
Garlic Shrimp, 197
Gastric banding surgery, 8-9, 26–32
absorption and, 14
changing way you eat, 27
diet following surgery, 29–32
eating slowly, 28

feeling hungry, 27
fluids with meals, avoid drinking, 28
ground or pureed foods, 30–31
new foods, introducing, 28
proteins importance, 28, 30
sugar-free liquids, 29–30
sugars and, 12–13
water, 29
Gastric bypass (GBP) surgery, 8-9, 16–26
antacid therapy, 24
appetite, 16–17
body, your new, 20
chewing gum and, 25
cramps, gas, or diarrhea, 17–18, 22
description of, 16
diet after, 20–26
dumping syndrome, 18–19
effects from, 16
exercise, 20
fluids, 21
food diary, 18
food groups, incorporating all, 26
hair loss, 19
lactose intolerance and, 12
low-fat, low-sugar solid foods, 25–26
protein goals, 20, 22–25
sample of day's diet, 24
stages of diet after surgery, 21–26
stomach, your new, 17–18
water, 21
weight loss, decrease in, 19–20
Greek High-Protein Berry-Licious
Milkshake, 57
Greek Salad, 114
Greek Scramble, 47
Greek Yogurt-Cucumber Sauce, 205
Green Bean Casserole, 153
Green Chili and Cheese Cornbread Muffins,
70
Green Tomato Soup with Fresh Tarragon,
93
Grilled Salmon with Toasted Fennel and
Paprika, 190
Ground Beef and Spinach Scramble, 46
Guidelines, 10–15
carbohydrates, 12
fats, 13
fiber, 13–14
fluids, 10–11
protein, 11–12
sugars, 12–13
vitamins and minerals, 14–15

H
Hearts of Palm with Arugula and
Endive Salad, 111
Heather's Tasty Marinara Sauce, 203
Herb and Cheese Mashed Cauliflower, 162
Holiday Pumpkin Parfait, 231
Horseradish Dressing, 129
Hot Artichoke Dip, 135

I
Italian Scramble, 49

J
Juice guidelines, 10

K
Knives, 42
Kosher Lamb Souvlaki, 204

L
Lamb
Kosher Lamb Souvlaki, 204
Latkes, 141
Lavender-Blueberry Muffins, 67
Leftover Salmon Salad, 115
Leftover Salmon Sandwich, 81
Lemon-Barbecue Meatloaf, 201
Lemon Sorbet, 228
Lemons, importance of, 43
Lentil Soup, 99
Lentils, note about, 99
Lobster and Scallop Sauté with Fresh
Steamed Green Beans, 180
Lunches, 73–91
Asian Chicken Wrap, 86
Avocado, Cream Cheese, and Bacon
Sandwich, 76
Awesome Egg Salad Sandwich, 82
Bacon, Tomato, Lettuce, and Cream
Cheese Sandwich, 82
Baked Ham and Cheese Sandwich, 80
Best Ever Tofu Burger, 83
Classic Turkey, Cranberry, and Cream
Cheese Sandwich, 78
Classic Turkey and Swiss Wrap, 74
Cumin Mushroom Quesadillas, 73
Fresh Mozzarella, Tomato, and
Tapenade Sandwich, 80
Leftover Salmon Sandwich, 81
Mediterranean Chicken Salad Sandwich,
77
Pita Pizza, 89
Simple Sloppy Joe, 90
Spinach-Turkey Wraps, 75
Tuna Salad Wrap to Go, 91
Turkey Sandwich with Cucumbers and
Herbed Creamed Cheese, 81
Ultimate Veggie Sandwich, 79
Zesty Turkey Burger Pita Pocket, 85

M
Mandarin Orange Broccoli, 159
Mandarin Pea Pod Salad, 108
Maria and Karen's Zesty Lemon and Caper
Chicken, 193
Marinated Mushroom and Tomato Salad
with Dijon Vinaigrette, 112
Marinated Vegetable Salad in Creamy
Vinaigrette, 120
Mark's Fruity French Toast, 52
Mediterranean Chicken Salad Sandwich, 77
Mexican Shrimp Salad with Jicama, 113
Mexican Turkey Skillet Casserole, 206
Mixing bowls, 42
Muffins
Bacon-Cheddar Muffins, 72
Carrot Muffins with Fresh Dill, 68
Fresh Strawberry Muffins, 69
Green Chili and Cheese Cornbread
Muffins, 70
Lavender-Blueberry Muffins, 67
Spring Herb and Zucchini Muffins, 66
Zucchini-Bran Muffins, 71
Mushroom and Swiss Cheese Scramble, 47
Mushrooms
Chicken, Broccoli, and Mushroom
Casserole, 195
Chicken Curry with Fresh Mint and
Shiitake Mushrooms, 217
Cumin Mushroom Omelet, 54

Cumin Mushroom Quesadillas, 73
Marinated Mushroom and Tomato Salad with Dijon Vinaigrette, 112
Mushroom and Swiss Cheese Scramble, 47
Pita Pizza, 89
Savory Ground Turkey Meat Loaf, 202
Spanish Omelet, 50
Stuffed Mushrooms, 145
Mustard Rub, 172

O
One Pot Chicken Dinner in a Pinch, 207

P
Pacific Dungeness Crab Cakes, 143
Pasta
Mexican Turkey Skillet Casserole, 206
Whole-Wheat Elbow Macaroni Salad, 106
Pepper in your diet, 43, 178
Pita Pizza, 89
Plum Tomatoes with Blue Cheese, 144
Pork
Curried Pork Loin Roast with Currants, Apples, and Sweet Onions, 178-179
Pork Roast Dry Rub, 172
Pork Roast Rub, 170
Pork Tenderloin Medallions with Spanish Smoked Paprika, 175
Pork Roast Dry Rub, 172
Pork Roast Rub, 170
Pork Tenderloin Medallions with Spanish Smoked Paprika, 175
Postoperative nutrition guide, early, 16–43
biliopancreatic diversion. See Biliopancreatic diversion
gastric banding surgery. See Gastric banding surgery
gastric bypass surgery. See Gastric bypass surgery
Pot Roast á la Sara, 198
Potato Leek Soup with Fresh Tarragon, 102
Potatoes
Boiled New Potatoes with Fresh Parsley, 165
Latkes, 141
One Pot Chicken Dinner in a Pinch, 207
Pot Roast á la Sara, 198
Potato Leek Soup with Fresh Tarragon, 102
Sweet Potato Soup, 104
Sweet Potatoes au Gratin, 166
Vegetarian Shepherd's Pie, 225
Vegetarian Vegetable Soup, 105
Whole Roasted Chicken with Potatoes and Brussels Sprouts, 176
Zucchini and Potato Strata, 65
Pots and pans, 42
Poultry. See Chicken; Turkey
Protein powders, 40–41
Berry Delicious Cream of Wheat, 55
egg, 41
Frozen Fruit Smoothie, 58
Greek High-Protein Berry-Licious Milkshake, 57
rice, 40
soy, 41
Vegetarian Vegetable Soup, 105
whey, 40

Protein
foods high in, 12
goals after biliopancreatic diversion surgery, 34–35
goals after gastric banding surgery, 28–29, 30
goals after gastric bypass surgery, 20, 22–25
guidelines, 11–12

R
Radicchio and Cauliflower Salad with Roasted Walnuts, 116
Rice
protein powder, 40
Spanish Shrimp with Jasmine Rice and Green Beans, 214
Roasted Asparagus with Crispy Bacon, 152
Roasted Beets and Mango Salad, 119
Roasted Garlic, 136
Roasted Veal and Shallots and Fennel, 210
Rubs for meats and poultry, dry, 170–174
Cajun Blackened Rub, 171
Curry Dry Rub, 173
Dill Rub, 170
Dry Jamaican Jerk Rub, 171
Ethiopian Spice Mix, 174
Fearsome Garlic Port Rub, 174
Mustard Rub, 172
Pork Roast Dry Rub, 172
Pork Roast Rub, 170
Tandoori Dry Rub, 173

S
Salads and dressings, 106–129
Asian-Influenced Cabbage Medley, 123
Blue Cheese Dressing, 126
Classic Spinach Salad with Apple Cider Vinaigrette, 107
Creamy Italian Dressing, 127
Creamy Lemon Herb Dressing, 126
Dill Dressing, 129
French Dressing, 127
Fresh Fruit Salad, 121
Garden Goddess Dressing, 128
Greek Salad, 114
Hearts of Palm with Arugula and Endive Salad, 111
Horseradish Dressing, 129
Leftover Salmon Salad, 115
Mandarin Pea Pod Salad, 108
Marinated Mushroom and Tomato Salad with Dijon Vinaigrette, 112
Marinated Vegetable Salad in Creamy Vinaigrette, 120
Mexican Shrimp Salad with Jicama, 113
Radicchio and Cauliflower Salad with Roasted Walnuts, 116
Roasted Beets and Mango Salad, 119
Sweet and Sour Marinated Cucumbers, 122
Sweet Lemon Poppy Seed Dressing, 128
Thousand Island Dressing, 113
Watercress Salad with Tarragon and Mint Leaves, 124
Whole-Wheat Elbow Macaroni Salad, 106
Salt in diet, 42
Sandwiches
Asian Chicken Wrap, 86

Avocado, Cream Cheese, and Bacon Sandwich, 76
Awesome Egg Salad Sandwich, 82
Bacon, Tomato, Lettuce, and Cream Cheese Sandwich, 82
Baked Ham and Cheese Sandwich, 80
Best Ever Tofu Burger, 83
Classic Turkey, Cranberry, and Cream Cheese Sandwich, 78
Classic Turkey and Swiss Wrap, 74
Fresh Mozzarella, Tomato, and Tapenade Sandwich, 80
Leftover Salmon Sandwich, 81
Mediterranean Chicken Salad Sandwich, 77
Spinach-Turkey Wraps, 75
Tuna Salad Wrap to Go, 91
Turkey Sandwich with Cucumbers and Herbed Cream Cheese, 81
Ultimate Veggie Sandwich, 79
Zesty Turkey Burger Pita Pocket, 85
Sanitizing work surfaces, 43
Sauces
Chive-Yogurt Sauce, 63
Greek Yogurt-Cucumber Sauce, 205
Heather's Tasty Marinara Sauce, 203
Spaghetti Squash with Pomodoro Sauce, 222
Savory Broccoli and Cheese Bread Pudding, 61
Savory Ground Turkey Meat Loaf, 202
Seafood
Baked Sea Bass, 186
Breaded Grouper Fillets, 181
Fillet of Salmon á la Herman, 189
Fillet of Salmon with Sesame-Orange Glaze, 185
Fillet of Sole with Vegetables Baked in Parchment, 183
Fresh Citrus Grilled Shrimp, 184
Garlic Shrimp, 196
Grilled Salmon with Toasted Fennel and Paprika, 190
Leftover Salmon Salad, 115
Leftover Salmon Sandwich, 81
Lobster and Scallop Sauté with Fresh Steamed Green Beans, 180
Mexican Shrimp Salad with Jicama, 113
Pacific Dungeness Crab Cakes, 143
salmon, wild versus farmed, 191
Smoked Salmon Dip, 140
Spanish Shrimp with Jasmine Rice and Green Beans, 214
Tuna Salad Wrap to Go, 91
Shears, kitchen, 42
Simple Sloppy Joe, 90
Slow-Cooked Bone-In White Chicken Chili, 192
Slow-Cooked Sausage and Lentil Stew, 208
Smoked Salmon Dip, 140
Soups, 92–105
Black Bean Soup, 101
Chilled Honeydew Soup with Spearmint, 96
Creamy Tomato Parmesan Soup, 100
Curried Carrot Soup, 92
Fall Harvest Pumpkin Soup, 95
Green Tomato Soup with Fresh Tarragon, 93
Lentil Soup, 99

Potato Leek Soup with Fresh Tarragon, 102
Sweet Potato Soup, 104
Vegetarian Vegetable Soup, 105
Southwestern Marinated Chicken Breast, 211
Soy protein powder, 41
Spaghetti Squash with Pomodoro Sauce, 222
Spanish Omelet, 50
Spanish Shrimp with Jasmine Rice and Green Beans, 214
Spinach
    Asian Chicken Wrap, 86
    Classic Spinach Salad with Apple Cider Vinaigrette, 107
    Easy and Delicious Spinach Dip, 138
    Ground Beef and Spinach Scramble, 46
    Mandarin Pea Pod Salad, 108
    Slow-Cooked Sausage and Lentil Stew, 208
    Spinach-Turkey Wraps, 75
    Tasty Baked Tofu with Sautéed Spinach, 226
    Tuna Salad Wrap to Go, 91
Spinach-Turkey Wraps, 75
Spring Herb and Zucchini Muffins, 66
Steamed Asparagus Lemonata, 158
Stocking kitchen tips, 42–43
Strainer or sieve, 42
Stuffed Mushrooms, 145
Sugar-Free Ginger Applesauce Cake, 229
Sugar substitutes. See Artificial sweeteners
Sugar guidelines, 12–13
Sweet and Sour Marinated Cucumbers, 122
Sweet Corn Relish, 130
Sweet Lemon Poppy Seed Dressing, 128
Sweet Potato Soup, 104
Sweet Potatoes au Gratin, 166
Sweeteners, artificial. See Artificial sweeteners

T
Tandoori Dry Rub, 173
Tasty Baked Tofu with Sautéed Spinach, 226
Toasted Pita Chips, 136
Tools for the kitchen, tips for, 42–43
Tomato and Fresh Basil Scramble, 48
Tomatoes, how to peel, 105
Traditional Hummus, 146
Tuna Salad Wrap to Go, 91
Turkey
    All-American Scramble, 44
    Bacon, Tomato, Lettuce, and Cream Cheese Sandwich, 82
    Bacon-Cheddar Muffins, 72
    Baked Ham and Cheese Sandwich, variation, 80
    Breakfast Turkey Sausage Patties, 62
    Classic Turkey, Cranberry, and Cream Cheese Sandwich, 78
    Classic Turkey and Swiss Wrap, 74
    Mexican Turkey Skillet Casserole, 206
    Pita Pizza variation, 89
    Roasted Asparagus with Crispy Bacon, 152
    Savory Ground Turkey Meat Loaf, 202
    Slow-Cooked Sausage and Lentil Stew, 208
    Spinach-Turkey Wraps, 75

Turkey Sandwich with Cucumbers and Herbed Cream Cheese, 81
Zesty Turkey Burger Pita Pocket, 85
Zucchini, Bacon, and Swiss Cheese Scramble, 48
Turkey Sandwich with Cucumbers and Herbed Cream Cheese, 81

U
Ultimate Veggie Sandwich, 79

V
Vegetable Party Platter, 130
Vegetables. See also Beans; Broccoli; Mushrooms; Potatoes; Spinach
    Asian Chicken Wrap, 86
    Asian-Influenced Cabbage Medley, 123
    Brussels Hash, 149
    Carrot Muffins with Fresh Dill, 68
    Citrus-Roasted Carrots with Honey, 169
    Curried Carrot Soup, 92
    Curried Pork Loin Roast with Currants, Apples, and Sweet Onions, 178-179
    Eggplant Parmesan, 221
    Fall Harvest Pumpkin Soup, 95
    Fillet of Sole with Vegetables Baked in Parchment, 183
    Herb and Cheese Mashed Cauliflower, 162
    Holiday Pumpkin Parfait, 231
    Hot Artichoke Dip, 135
    Lentil Soup, 99
    Mandarin Pea Pod Salad, 108
    Marinated Vegetable Salad in Creamy Vinaigrette, 120
    One Pot Chicken Dinner in a Pinch, 207
    Pot Roast á la Sara, 198
    Radicchio and Cauliflower Salad with Roasted Walnuts, 116
    Roasted Asparagus with Crispy Bacon, 152
    Roasted Beets and Mango Salad, 119
    Roasted Garlic, 136
    Slow-Cooked Sausage and Lentil Stew, 208
    Spaghetti Squash with Pomodoro Sauce, 222
    Spanish Omelet, 50
    Spring Herb and Zucchini Muffins, 66
    Steamed Asparagus Lemonata, 158
    Sweet and Sour Marinated Cucumbers, 122
    Sweet Corn Relish, 130
    Ultimate Veggie Sandwich, 79
    Vegetable Party Platter, 130
    Vegetarian Shepherd's Pie, 225
    Vegetarian Vegetable Soup, 105
    Whole Roasted Chicken with Potatoes and Brussels Sprouts, 176
    Zucchini, Bacon, and Swiss Cheese Scramble, 48
    Zucchini and Potato Strata, 65
    Zucchini-Bran Muffins, 71
    Zucchini Frittata with Capers and Olives, 63
Vegetarian Shepherd's Pie, 225
Vegetarian Vegetable Soup, 105
Vinaigrettes
    Classic Spinach Salad with Apple Cider Vinaigrette, 107
    Marinated Mushroom and Tomato Salad

with Dijon Vinaigrette, 112
Marinated Vegetable Salad in Creamy Vinaigrette, 120
Vitamins and minerals guidelines, 14–15, 33

W
Water guidelines, 10
Watercress Salad with Tarragon and Mint Leaves, 124
Whey protein powder, 40
Whole Roasted Chicken with Potatoes and Brussels Sprouts, 176–177
Whole-Wheat Elbow Macaroni Salad, 106
Wine, 43

Y
Yogurt
    Carrot Muffins with Fresh Dill, 68
    Chicken Curry with Fresh Mint and Shiitake Mushrooms, 217
    Chive-Yogurt Sauce, 63
    Creamy Tomato Parmesan Soup, 100
    Curry Yogurt Dip, 131
    Greek High-Protein Berry-Licious Milkshake, 57
    Greek Yogurt-Cucumber Sauce, 205
    Green Tomato Soup with Fresh Tarragon, 93
    Lavender-Blueberry Muffins, 67
    Marinated Vegetable Salad in Creamy Vinaigrette, 120
    Mexican Shrimp Salad with Jicama, 113
    Spring Herb and Zucchini Muffins, 66
    Zucchini-Bran Muffins, 71

Z
Zesty Broiled Marinated Chicken, 213
Zesty Turkey Burger Pita Pocket, 85
Zucchini and Potato Strata, 65
Zucchini Frittata with Capers and Olives, 63
Zucchini, Bacon, and Swiss Cheese Scramble, 48
Zucchini-Bran Muffins, 71

Acknowledgments

Lynette and I would first like to thank the wonderful staff at Fair Winds Press, including our editor, Wendy Gardner, and our marketing and publicity director, Mary Aarons. Without your boundless faith in us, belief in our vision, and endless support and patience, this project could not have happened. We thank you, from the bottom of our hearts, for giving us this opportunity to share and combine our expertise and love of nutrition and the culinary arts to create this book for weight-loss surgery patients. Thank you, also, to Rosalind Wanke and all of the professionals involved in taking such care to photograph our recipes. We really appreciate your attention to detail! Thanks also to our amazing copyeditor, Jennifer Reich.

I'd like to thank my family, including my parents, Ed and Sara, and Maria, Karen, and of course, Zoe, and Bette as well. You're very special to me, and I can't thank you enough for always believing in me and supporting this book. I appreciate the recipes you shared as well! I love you very, very much.

Thank you to my dear friend and coauthor, Lynette, for always being there for me while we developed and tested different recipe ideas and talked about the vision for our book. Although I was in Boston and you in Seattle, the endless phone conversations and e-mails back and forth to tweak the recipes to ensure they were tasty, yet healthy, seemed pretty painless because I knew your heart, as well as mine, was in this project from the start. I can't thank you enough for all of the love you have poured into our book. *Molto grazi*!

A big thank you to Dr. Scott Shikora, chief of the division of bariatric surgery, at Tufts-New England Medical Center. I've really enjoyed working together at NEMC, as well as on book chapters and speaking at conferences. Your tireless dedication to the field of bariatric surgery is admirable.

Thank you also to Dr. Paulo Pacheco, a successful gastroenterologist in New York City and a dear family friend. I appreciate your introducingthe manuscript to your friend and colleague, Dr. Christine Ren, a prominent bariatric surgeon in New York City, who then took an interest in it and was kind enough to offer to edit it. The comments were very much appreciated, and the insight regarding how your center, among others, may differ with respect to the diet progression after gastric banding, was truly priceless. Thank you, Dr. Ren.

And thank you to Linda Aills, R.D., for her help with our recipe testimonials.

I'd like to give a *big* thank you to all of my weight-loss surgery patients at NEMC. Although your names aren't mentioned to protect your privacy, please know that you were my inspiration for this book, and I dedicate it to all of you!

Cheers to nourishing the new you!

Margaret Furtado, M.S., R.D., L.D.N.

About the Authors

Margaret Furtado, M.S., R.D., L.D.N., a registered and licensed
dietitian/nutritionist with almost 20 years' clinical experience, is currently part of
the multidisciplinary team at the Massachusetts General Hospital (MGH) Weight
Center, where she counsels patients on both medical and surgical weight loss
(including gastric bypass and gastric banding procedures). Prior to working at MGH,
Ms. Furtado spent four years working at Tufts-New England Medical Center's
(NEMC) Obesity Consult Center, providing both individual and group consultations
for gastric bypass, gastric banding, and BPD surgery patients. It was while at NEMC
that she wrote *Recipes for Life After Weight-Loss Surgery.* Ms. Furtado earned her mas-
ter's degree in nutrition and dietetics at Florida International University in Miami,
and her bachelor of science degree in nutrition and dietetics from the University of
Rhode Island. Ms. Furtado lectures across the country on issues pertaining to
weight-loss surgery.

Lynette Schultz, chef, L.R.C.P., R.T., received her culinary training at various
venues around the Seattle area. She currently works as a guest chef at Hedgebrook, a
retreat for women writers near her home on Whidbey Island, Washington, and as a
licensed respiratory care practitioner at Whidbey General Hospital.